SO-APM-987

HOW TO DO BUSINESS TAX FREE

By

Midas Malone

How to do Business Tax Free

First Printing—January, 1976

Second Printing (Revised)—June, 1976

Third Printing (Revised)—Quality Paperback Edition—April, 1980

© 1980 by Midas Malone

All rights reserved. No part of this book, except

for brief passages in articles and reviews that refer to

author and publisher, may be reproduced without written

permission of the Publisher.

Library of Congress Number—75-45877

ISBN—0-913864-45-5

Published by

Enterprise Publishing Inc.
725 Market Street
Wilmington, Delaware 19701

Printed in the United States of America

TABLE OF CONTENTS

"Taxation is Theft"

Author Unknown

"Government is not reason, it is not eloquence—it is force. Like fire it is a dangerous servant and a fearful master; never for a moment should it be left to irresponsible action."

George Washington

Each of us has a duty to himself to safeguard the money (property) he has earned. We have an equal duty to avoid providing means to those who wish to enslave us. When your earnings go toward taxes they are entrusted to the government. No modern government in the world has yet earned our trust. Government bureaucrats all seek more power and their own reelection. Tax money taken against our wishes by force fuels that power. Direct and indirect taxes in the U.S. are approaching half our income and rising. When societies reach this 50% mark, according to history's barometer, economic and social collapse follow.

Tax money is often used against our interests. Examples include sending young men to die in unnecessary political wars, welfare to millions of able-bodied persons, punishment of victimless crimes, vast waste, and a continuing unchecked expansion on the size of every level of government (including more tax collectors!) We have no control over how our money is spent. Let us recognize that every penny we pay in taxes may properly be looked at as fuel used for the purpose of our own self-destruction.

You who share with me the love of the principles of individual freedom and limited government may wish to do everything possible to achieve the only moral political system based on man's nature—laissez faire capitalism. Under such a system government would be small and highly limited in power. Its only activities would be protecting individual rights. Fundamentally there are only two ways individual rights can be violated—force and fraud. Because of this, therein would be the *only* legitimate government functions. Tax contributions would be *voluntary* and used for government services rendered. Those who chose to support their government and make contributions would receive the major benefits i.e. courts, etc. Non-contributors would not receive many of the government services.

I am committed toward the struggle of effecting positive political changes toward this final goal. Won't you think about this and consider joining me? In the meantime, it is my hope this book will be useful to you.

Midas Malone

Introduction

Why we are here

The year 1973 will one day rank in history with 1929. In 1929 the world turned upside down, and before it finally flipped back over to a stance of relative economic equilibrium, basic changes had occurred in our relationships with our national government and, as a consequence, in our lives. In 1973 another convulsion sent a shock wave through our national and individual systems; and while the total effects will not be registered for years—perhaps generations—the immediate effects are profound.

Actually, historians of the future may rightfully designate 1933 as the year that really started the cataclysm. The storm that broke over us late in 1973 with the Arab nations' sudden oil embargo, followed by quadrupled crude oil prices after the embargo was lifted, only exacerbated a problem that had been gestating for years. And that is the problem of irresponsible government interference with the natural forces and balances of a once free economy.

Just when the moment of conception occurred is debatable. Some contend it was the Depression that made us ripe for a Franklin Roosevelt and his Rubber Stamp Congress. Others say it was a Las Vegas mentality in the stock market that brought on the crash. Still other schools of thought attribute the setting of our present economic course to more subtle and complex, even sinister, factors. In any event, the die was cast in 1933 when we went off the Gold Standard. That removed the traditional restraints against putting into circulation more paper money than its equivalent in the total real wealth of the nation. Everyone needs discipline. And gold provided the self-discipline we needed to keep us from spending more money than we had to spend. As long as U.S. paper dollars were at least theoretically redeemable in their face value of gold or silver, the powerful psychological effect of those precious metals in our treasury provided the restraint that insured a dollar's worth of purchasing power for each dollar in circulation.

Without the historic, almost mystical, power of gold providing a rigid control on the quantity of bills we could print, there remained only America's national maturity and integrity as a basis for world-wide confidence in the dollar. For a relatively long time this appeared to be more or less adequate. The new dollar was able to ride for a while on the reputation of its former self. But it could last only for a while. Politics and biennial elections tempted too many ambitious office-seekers to play fast and loose with the economic principles that had brought the U.S. to the pinnacle of productivity and personal gain for its citizens. The common man could understand an explanation of public spending limited by the supply of gold. Without that higher power holding the brakes on government spending, the subject became so complicated for him he was quite willing to entrust the matter to self-proclaimed specialists in that field who promised a better life in return for his vote. So much easier to choose the candidate who assured him that he deserved better than he was getting, and that the government should give it to him. Easier than choosing the candidate who urged prudence and self-denial to keep the budget balanced.

And so the pattern was set: politicians buying office with promises of handouts; voters not knowing where the money was coming from, certainly now knowing that it was coming from them; and growing expenditures followed by increasing demands and exorbitant promises; and so on in an ever-rising spiral. It is always far easier to spend money than to earn it. The new generation of socioeconomic thinking simply bridged the gap between demand and supply by sending the bill to the government. The government, however, had the same problem of easy-demand, hard-supply. Since it would not send the bill back marked "insufficient funds," it was left two options, and it had to exercise both: raise taxes as fast as the traffic would bear, and borrow the remainder.

There were voices of caution and of alarm, but they were dismissed as the reactionary cries of the wealthy who had more than was moral and were merely defending their sinful interests. "Soak the rich" made sense to the teeming millions, as did the blandishment to rationalize the soaring national debt: "What's the difference? We only owe it to ourselves!"

How fortunate that such arguments made sense to the majority vote, fortunate for a new elite that came of age during the World War II emergency: the federal bureaucrat. Fostered by an atmosphere that named federal money as a panacea for all problems, that condoned direct government competition with free enterprise under rules written by the government, that encouraged bureaucratic growth by rewarding growth with more power, the bureaucracy burgeoned.

Like youth on a binge, it made very good sense to all but a few, who were looked upon as the scolding voices of an older generation reared on out-moded ideas. The analogy of a drug or alcoholic high, in fact, is not too far-fetched. The initial sensation is one of giddy pleasure and surprise. With time, more of the drug is required to achieve the same euphoric sensation. Then one day, with grave uneasiness, the subject realizes there is a heavy price tag on his frivolity. He is heavily in debt, his health is failing, his reputation is suffering, and he can't seem to do anything about it. He is hooked. He is faced with the prospect of going on in the same direction down to oblivion, or taking the cure and suffering the pain and anguish of withdrawal.

The economies of the United States and of the other relatively unfettered nations who are necessarily affected by the U.S. economy have heard the whistle blow. The pyramid has collapsed. The party is over. The light of dawn tells us that the rich are not the ones paying the bills. We see that huge sums of money have been spent foolishly. Through the hangover we begin to see that the good-time Charlies have been buying drinks and entertainment with our money, not theirs and not someone else's. And like a muscle-flexing bouncer, our national commitments stand before us demanding payment. Those of us who are sober enough, realize that we have been taken. The glib politicians were not interested in our welfare after all, but in winning another term of office. They were not the experts we thought they were, either. Through a lack of will, through ignorance, negligence or even malice, they deluded us. And we feel embittered by the realization that we too were responsible because we did not check up on the claims made, did not analyze the results. We of the middle class were too trusting and too lazy.

After all, a special education is not required to understand that only one dollar can be put into circulation for every dollar's worth of goods or services. If the government issues a second dollar for that same dollar's worth of goods or services, the dollars might say one dollar on their face, but they are really worth only fifty cents each (or one dollar is still worth a dollar and the other is worth nothing, and their average purchasing power is fifty cents). That, we learned, is what causes inflation: more money in circulation than there is productivity to supply the total face value. Now we see that the winning of more money for less work has been a hollow victory. We lose after all. It is we—overwhelmingly the middle class—who must lend money to the government to pay the interest on money the government has already borrowed from us. And then we must pay the higher interest rates brought on by a small supply of capital when we borrow for our own private financial needs—which often arise because our after-tax income cannot supply the required capital. It is also we who must pay an ever-rising cost of welfare, while also paying the cost of defending us all against potential enemies who would subvert or crush us. Potential enemies to whom we sell wheat because their system and their concentration on weapons fail to provide the food they need, and then higher prices for our wheat products because of the reduced supply. It is the same kind of nonsense as in years past when we paid to increase farm productivity at the same time we were paying farmers not to produce; paid subsidies to farmers, then paid to store the surplus food; paid the higher prices at the supermarket caused by reducing the supply; and finally paid the cost of dumping the food that stayed too long in storage.

Regardless of who caused the waste or made the mistake, the bulk of the bill was paid by the man in the middle—the middle income group—through a variety of taxes, including the most vicious of all, perhaps: inflation. Admittedly, inflation is one tax that all levels pay; and ironically it is caused by the very spendthrift politicians who are put into office by the poor people who think they are being helped. Still, the great burden has been borne by middle income taxpayers.

This is not to say that the middle income Everyman has been openly complaining. If he had been, we would not be in the state we are in today, for after all, the squeaky wheel does get the grease. All the time that the political activists have been noisily pushing social contributions to the lower class, and the wealthy class members have been quietly maneuvering to protect their capital, middle class Everyman has been plodding along his dutiful way, trusting in himself and in his institutions to see him through. But little by little, then more and more, into his consciousness has crept a vague—at moments acute—feeling of anxiety.

Reared in the ethic that hard work, consideration for others, and faith in God and country would ultimately and always reward its practitioners, the middle class man studied and worked and invested, voted for his party's nominees, contributed to worthy causes, fought and sacrificed against external challenges, enjoyed life in a variety of simple ways, and paid his taxes.

The recurring twinges of anxiety troubled him because he could not bring their source into sharp focus. He clearly seemed to be gaining material assets. But each year his taxes were increasing also. So were prices. So was his personal debt from charge purchases and loans. And so, he read, was the national debt. Was he really gaining, he asked himself, or was he just borrowing against the future? Should he feel guilty for grumbling about taxes when they said the money was needed to elevate society in general and the poor in particular? If a majority of his elected representatives voted periodically to raise taxes and the national debt ceiling to accommodate accelerating government spending, was it necessary for him to worry or try to take action? And what action could he take that would make any difference? Besides, he reasoned, those people know a lot more about such things than I do, and they wouldn't let us go down the drain! Or would they?

Periodically from year to year, Mr. Middleclass would go through such mental exercises. His relief always came from his latest pay raise, a new outboard engine, or preoccupation with the myriad details associated with earning a living and rearing a family.

Still, the underlying worries remained and slowly grew, peaking like a small eruption at property reassessment and tax-filing time and every January as, suddenly, the FICA bite left a hole in his paycheck that had not been there for several months, and now was bigger than ever before. His fears accelerated as the social activists grew more aggressive and demanded more of his earnings while reports told of tax money for color television, for subsidized vacations he couldn't afford for himself, and for illegitimate propagation. He felt further frustrated and let down on learning that the nation's wealthy almost never pay the percentages of taxes shown on the progressive tax tables—that many persons receiving incomes several times the size of his own — pay lower taxes than he, or none at all.

Finally with a rush his ambivalence evaporated, his confidence in the omniscience of government leaders dissolved, and for the first time he viewed the total scene. The new perspective was grimly shocking. He saw every other element in his universe buying but not paying—the lower class, the upper class, the government, foreign nations—all withdrawing money to make purchases, while his element in the middle was really the only one making any deposits. And it appeared to be getting nothing but abuse for its efforts.

We are not here to defend these observations against the usual intellectual rejoiners, but to present them as a fact of our times. Government bureaucracy and government spending at all levels *have* been growing steadily; welfare payments *have* been rising; deficit spending *is* automatic in effect, and increasing; a babble of contentious voices *cannot* agree on how to stop inflation or conserve energy; and taxes *are* the largest single obstacle against maintaining a moderate living standard.

Everyone except the middle classman has an organization, a political faction, or a staff of experts to rely on for support. He does not have a block of votes, a large capital reserve, or the knowledge, experience, and sophistication that would enable him to defend himself. Yet if help is to be had, from where is it to come if not from himself? The concept is not new to him. Long ago he learned the basic rule that if you want a job done right, on time, and at a reasonable price, you have to do it yourself. So middle Everyman has taught himself to fix washing machines and television sets, install lighting fixtures and attic fans, hang wallpaper and draperies, lay floor coverings and paving, trouble-shoot furnaces and air conditioners, and even build garages, porches and houses. The how-to for his installation and maintenance needs has come to him in books, articles, courses, friendly neighbors, TV programs. For coping with his children's educational deficits and his local government, he has associations to provide him with information and a vehicle for concerted action.

But if he cannot get his state or federal government to balance their budgets—limit spending to actual revenues—and if he does not believe that any except the wealthy can avoid taxation on top of taxation, what is he to do?

It seems ridiculous that a great majority in this country cannot receive justice. It would appear that the majority could have anything it wanted. Second thoughts, though, remind us that organized minorities will almost always prevail over unorganized majorities. And even though there are signs that a middle class revolt is under way, there is still no real sign that the revolt is at last becoming organized. Granted a large number of the middle class majority might coalesce into a directed force (never in history has a conclusive political or social event been brought about by other than a minority of activists), it will take a relatively long time to produce fundamental changes and trend reversals. Nevertheless, in the final analysis, political action by a force representing the majority is probably the only lasting solution to the present delemma and the only hope for a free and solvent nation.

Meanwhile, is there anything our exasperated taxpayer can do as an individual to gain relief legally for himself in the near future? To virtually every problem there is a solution. All that is needed is discovery: If a solution is not immediately apparent, perseverance eventually will discover one. Since the whole problem came to a head in 1973, enough members of the mid-level income group have discovered they have a problem peculiar to their level, and searches for a solution have been conducted in earnest.

This book presents a solution.

The author has thoroughly researched the subject of tax havens and has concluded that they are not exclusively for the rich to shelter their capital from predatory collectors of taxes. That traditional assumption is based solely on the simple absence of any investigation otherwise. The book is, as far as the author knows, the first revelation of tax havens for modest capital sums.

What this means is that now the person who wants to protect $50,000 or $5,000 or who wants to operate a small or medium-size business,can follow the same routes taken by large companies, trusts, and wealthy individuals in legally avoiding the payment of taxes they would otherwise have to pay.

Tony Barbiere, owner of a four-chair barber shop, or Horace Weatherby, one pea in the corporation stew, can read this book and immediately start moving some of his   gainful resources toward a tax-free haven. This book does not say you should or should not do anything. It does not, because whatever course you follow has to be your own choice. There is, after all, some risk in anything you might do. The concepts in this book, however, will bring you as close to the ideal balance between gain and risk as you are likely to get anywhere.

Consider the alternative: You know that any capital gains generated in the U.S. will be taxed. In fact, any money a U.S. citizen makes anywhere in the world can be subject to tax. And between taxes and inflation, your net is hardly any gain at all. What it comes down to is that your present situation is a tried and proved stalemate at best, whereas any of a selection of other courses have been tried and proved effective in letting dollars grow unhindered by taxes.

The long trend toward hyperactive government has reached a point that calls for new thinking and different courses of action by overtaxed payers in the middle brackets seeking revived incentives for themselves and restored justice and common sense for their governments. With hardly greater provocation, American colonists once dumped tea into Boston harbor and ultimately revolted openly. Certainly we hope that common sense will regain the upper hand in our present quandary before it reaches such a stage. Persons today who feel just as indignant about oppressive government and confiscatory taxation as their colonial forbears can find substantial relief that was not available to eighteenth-century Americans. There are veritable legions of affluent persons in the United States and all other parts of the world who have for years quietly protested unfair tax and economic policies of government by legally placing capital beyond the reach of tax collectors. Now you, the less-than-affluent, can do the same thing if you choose. This book will tell you, in detail, all you need to know in order to make your decision. Furthermore, it will furnish you with step-by-step options, with names, addresses, sample forms to fill out, and approximate costs involved, if you decide to follow the tax-haven course.

Many publications have covered the subject of tax havens. What is really different about this book is the financial level to which it is addressed. This book makes tax havens a practical consideration for persons with modest investments who would like to operate a business or otherwise earn tax-free capital gains. You will be instructed how to use the same resources as have sheltered the large tax refugees. Your eyes will probably be opened to a whole new world of financial activities you likely never knew existed. And you might feel uneasy as you contemplate joining a circle that moves easily over national boundaries in conducting business, in changing residence, in transferring funds. It will probably seem to be rather fast and mysterious company for a fellow who pulls weeds, reads the sports pages, and seldom travels beyond the nearest shore resort. It might even seem slightly unpatriotic. Rest assured, however, that this seemingly sophisticated circle is made up of humans whose only difference from you, really, has been their money and their determination to protect it. They just got their motivation earlier than you. Now you have yours. As for patriotism, decide for yourself whether standing for the founding principles of freedom from government oppression or for the policies and ideologies that now prevail make you the better patriot.

Either way, go on and pull your weeds, read what you like, be a homebody, and go on loving the principles that made your country great. Who knows, if you stick to them faithfully, and enough persons join you, the U.S. and the rest of the world might yet become free once more! If, after reading this book, you would like to put some of your hard-earned money into a tax haven, remember that you might well be helping your country while you help yourself. One way, if there is a way, to make the politicians stop buying votes with your dollars is to give them fewer dollars. They are quite used to having less money than the price of things they think we must buy, but a quiet revolt by millions they have always taken for granted might help shift matters back toward equilibrium, If not, a tidy nest egg tucked away safely would be a great comfort to you during a period of national economic calamity.

Or worse. Even the United States, the traditional bastion of strength, freedom, and wealth, the nation with the oldest written constitution in the world (and in recent years, the most tortured), does not have a guarantee from Heaven for survival under all circumstances. Haven't other nations lost their freedom to totalitarian governments when they did not maintain their ideals and their economic strength? Didn't Germany and Russia after World War I? Didn't Rome, the colossus of the ancient world, decay and finally collapse when it abandoned its principles and lost its sense of purpose? The final downfall of Rome, remember, occurred when public spending and taxation finally reached 50 percent of gross national product; just before the end, Romans were paying half their income in taxes. There were, of course, many facets behind Rome's demise. The U.S., too, is subject to many variables, but one of them is a steadily rising tax collection that, in all its many forms and at all levels of government, is approaching 50 percent. If history repeats itself, and—God forbid—your nation goes under, escape from politico-economic chaos and tyranny will take money, safely waiting for you in a tax haven you perhaps selected after reading this book.

But sink, swim, or tread water, you are going to learn something from this book that could be profoundly helpful to you.

1 Introduction To The Law Of Tax Havens

What follows is a general discussion of the law governing what you might call "tax haven corporations". These corporations are actually referred to in the tax law as "controlled foreign corporations," or "CFCs."

A CFC is a foreign corporation "controlled" by "U.S. persons." These persons are *also* "U.S. shareholders." The words in quotes in the preceding sentences are all specifically defined by the Internal Revenue Code. As you will see, the rules are fairly complex.

- A "U.S. person" is a citizen of the United States, a resident of the United States, a domestic partnership, domestic corporation, or an estate or trust whose foreign income is subject to U.S. tax.
- A "U.S. shareholder" is a "U.S. person" who owns at least 10% of the total combined voting power of all classes of stock entitled to vote in a foreign corporation. A. "U.S. person" who owns at least 10% of the total combined voting power of all classes of stock entitled to vote in a foreign corporation. A "U.S. person" is considered by the law to own 10% or more of the combined voting power if the person owns at least 20% of a class of shares of stock that has certain powers of control over the corporation.

A foreign corporation is a CFC if more than 50% of the voting power of all classes of stock entitled to vote is owned or is "considered" as owned (through "attribution of ownership" rules, to be discussed) by U.S. shareholders on *any* day during the tax year in question. So, the foreign corporation is a CFC if "U.S. persons" owning more than 10% of the voting stock *together* own more than 50% of the voting stock.

Right now, it may look as if Congress had boxed you in. It seems that if you own a substantial amount of stock, the income of your foreign corporation (classified as a CFC, unfortunately) is taxed. But let us consider a hypothetical example. It is really not as bleak as it looks:

A foreign corporation that *is* a CFC has a stock ownership pattern such as this one:

Manny owns 11%
Moe owns 11%
Jack owns 11%   Tristan, a German national
Bonnie owns 11%   owns 45%
Clyde owns 11%
(all of these shareholders are U.S. citizens)

This foreign corporation is a CFC because Manny, Moe, Jack, Bonnie, and Clyde, all being U.S. citizens, qualify as "U.S. persons;" *and* each of these U.S. persons own more than 10% of the voting stock of the foreign corporation. *And* all of the U.S. persons *together* own more than 50% (55% to be exact) of the voting stock of the corporation. Because the foreign corporation is a CFC, the corporation's undistributed earnings are subject to tax (if the earnings are distributed as dividends, of course, the recipients of the dividends are taxed on what each receives).

But Consider The Following:
A foreign corporation that is *not* a CFC has a shareholder structure such as this one:

Abbott owns 11%
Costello owns 11%
Burns owns 11%   Isolde, a German national,
Allen owns 11%   owns 47%
Harpo owns 9%
(all of these shareholders are U.S. citizens)

This foreign corporation is *not* a CFC. How can that be, you might ask? All five U.S. citizens own, *together*, more than 50% (53% to be exact) of the voting stock of the corporation. Very true. *However*, U.S. persons *each* owning *more than 10%* of the stock do not *own* more than 50% of the voting stock of the corporation. Harpo owns 9%. This fact, in effect, gets the foreign corporation "off the hook" as far as CFC status is concerned.

All right, we've discussed the "10% aspect" of the CFC classification problem. What about the "50% aspect" of the CFC problem? In the eyes of the law, what constitutes "more than 50% of the total combined voting power" of the voting shares? As will become clear to you, some of the more obvious loopholes that probably occurred to you have been plugged. Treasury Regulation S1.957-1(b) is the chief loophole plugger in this area.

"United States shareholders of a foreign corporation will be deemed to own the requisite percentage of total combined voting power with respect to such corporation—

(i) If they have the power to elect, appoint, or replace a majority of that body of persons exercising, with respect to such corporation, the powers ordinarily exercised by the board of directors of a domestic corporation;

(ii) If any person or persons elected or designated by such shareholders have the power, where such shareholders have the power to elect exactly one-half of the members of such governing body of such foreign corporation, either to cast a vote deciding an evenly divided vote of such body or, for the duration of any deadlock which may arise, to exercise the powers ordinarily exercised by such governing body; or

(iii) If the powers which would ordinarily be exercised by the board of directors of a domestic corporation are exercised with respect to such foreign corporation by a person whom such shareholders have the power to elect, appoint, or replace.

(2) *Shifting of formal voting power.* Any arrangement to shift formal voting power away from United States shareholders of a foreign corporation will not be given effect if in reality voting power is retained. . . . if there is any agreement, whether ex-

pressed or implied, that any shareholder will not vote his stock or will vote it only in a specified manner, or that shareholders owning stock having not more than 50 percent of the total combined voting power will exercise voting power normally possessed by a majority of shareholders, then the nominal ownership of the voting power will be disregarded in determining which shareholders actually hold such voting power, and this determination will be made on the basis of such agreement."

In short, the obvious ways around the problem of having your foreign corporation classified as a CFC are pretty effectively blocked. The long and the short of the matter is that even your foreign nominees ("dummies") will be held to be your agents, assuming, of course that such facts can be proven.

It is a matter of speculation how evidence could be obtained on this matter unless you or your foreign nominees told the IRS. As a matter of practice, foreign nominees who talk business with persons outside the corporation aren't selected for similar positions in the future. Thus, asking a reputable source for recommendations as to prospective nominees might be a wise way to find reliable persons.

But Wait—there is something else you should know. Through what are called "attribution of ownership" rules, stock owned by one person or entity may be deemed to be legally owned by another person or entity.

Attribution of Ownership

There are two "attribution of ownership" rules which must concern each tax haven planner. The first is the "Chain of Ownership" rule, and the second is the "Constructive Ownership" rule.

Chain of Ownership Rule

This rule provides that stock is "owned" if "owned" directly or, importantly, "*indirectly*" (as defined by the tax law, of course). Thus, Regulation § 1.958-1(b) states that:

"Stock owned, directly or indirectly, by or for a foreign corporation, foreign partnership, or foreign trust or foreign estate. . .

shall be considered as being owned proportionately by its shareholders, partners, or beneficiaries, respectively. Stock considered to be owned by reason of the application of this paragraph shall, for purposes of reapplying this paragraph, be treated as actually owned by such person."

Regulation § 1.958-1(c) continues with a blanket statement designed to nullify the effect of clever devices to veil "true" ownership:

"Any arrangement which artificially decreases a United States person's proportionate interest will not be recognized."

Constructive Ownership Rule

This rule is slightly different in concept from the "Chain of Ownership" rule. Under the latter, the IRS *traces* owners to see who "really" owns stock. Under the "Constructive Ownership" rule, no tracing is done. Instead, an individual is considered to own stock if the stock is owned in name by a person or entity which stands in a close relationship with the individual.

There are several subparts to the "Constructive Ownership" rule:

(1) An *individual* is considered to own stock which is owned directly or indirectly by or for his/her spouse, children, grandchildren, and parents. EXCEPTION: Stock owned by a nonresident alien individual is not considered as owned by a United States citizen or resident alien individual;

(2) Stock owned directly or indirectly by or for a *partnership* or *estate* shall be considered as owned proportionately by its partners or beneficiaries. Conversely, stock owned directly or indirectly by or for a partner or beneficiary of an estate shall be considered as owned by the partnership or estate. IN ADDITION: If a partnership or estate owns directly or indirectly more than 50% of the total combined voting power of all classes of stock entitled to vote in a corporation, it shall be considered as owning *all* the stock entitled to vote;

(3) Stock owned directly or indirectly by or for a *trust* shall be considered as owned by its beneficiaries in proportion to the interest of the beneficiaries in the trust. Stock owned directly or indirectly by or for a beneficiary of a trust shall be considered as owned by the trust, *unless* such beneficiary's interest in the trust is remote and not vested (i.e., certain to vest). IN ADDITION: If a *trust* owns directly or indirectly more than 50% of the total combined voting power of all classes of stock entitled to vote in a *corporation*, it shall be considered as owning *all* of the stock entitled to vote;

(4) Stock owned directly or indirectly by or for any portion of a *trust*, which is in fact owned by the supposed *grantor* of the *trust*—in other words, where a "grantor" has not really surrendered his/her rights over the trust property, and therefore is really still the owner of the property—is considered to be still owned by the phony "grantor." Stock owned directly or indirectly by or for a person who is considered the owner of a trust (i.e., the phony "grantor") shall be considered as owned by the trust;

(5) If 10% or more in value of the stock in a *corporation* is owned directly or indirectly by or for any person, such person shall be considered as owning the stock owned directly or indirectly by or for such corporation, in that proportion which the value of the stock which such person so owns bears to the value of all the stock in such corporation. If 50% or more in value of the stock in a corporation is owned directly or indirectly by or for any person, such corporation shall be considered as owning the stock owned directly or indirectly by or for such person. (But this provision is not applied so as to consider a corporation as owning its own stock!)

There is only one reason why we have quoted these provisions at length. (We didn't do it to bore you!) We did it to illustrate the "bottom line" on this matter: if any individual or any entity "really" owns the stock of a foreign corporation, then that person or entity will be considered to be the "real" owner of the stock; The rules are circular, and they were intended to be that way. Thus, income, when distributed (and most of the time, even when undistributed), may be attributed to the person or entity with the "real" ownership interest. And *unless* a taxpayer has some of the garden variety (or exotic) deductions, exemptions, or credits available, tax will be due on that income.

Not all income of a CFC is taxable to its U.S. shareholder. The U.S. shareholders of a CFC are taxable only on "subpart F income"— referring to Subchapter N, Subpart F of the Internal Revenue Code.

There are four types of Subpart F income. Three types probably don't concern most of the readers of this book: income gained through activities constituting participation in an international boycott, money paid by a CFC to government officials which constitutes a bribe, kickback, or other illegal payment (i.e., the amount of money so paid is considered income *to* the CFC), and income from the insurance or reinsurance of U.S. risks.

The fourth type of income is "Foreign Base Company Income," which, in turn, has four subparts. These four subparts are:

(1) Foreign personal holding company income, including rents, royalties, dividends, interest, and gains from the sale or exchange of stock;

(2) Foreign base company income, gained from purchases of personal property from sales to related persons, trusts, partnerships, estates, or corporations, if the goods are produced or grown, and purchased or sold for use, in a country other than the one in which the foreign corporation is incorporated;

(3) Foreign base company service income, from compensation, commissions, fees, or otherwise, derived in connection with the performance of commercial and like services which are performed for, or on behalf of a related person, partnership, trust, estate, or corporation, and which are performed outside the country under the laws of which the CFC is created or organized;

(4) Foreign base company shipping income, from the use or

leasing for use of any aircraft or vessel in foreign commerce or from services directly related to this use, or from the sale or other disposition of such aircraft or vessel.

Frankly, the laws of the past years have considerably tightened up on the possibilities of escaping taxation through the tax haven route.

A Little Sunshine Amid The Gloom

It may seem from what you've read so far in this book that tax avoidance through the use of tax havens is virtually closed to you. We must concede that the letter of the law is fairly strict. We have included in this book a sometimes technical discussion of the law— even though it's pretty dreary—because we want you to be informed. The desire to be informed as to the rigors of the law in this area is one of the reasons why you bought this book, after all.

However, we think it is also fair that you take the sweet with the bitter.

Let us illustrate.

We know of a prominent attorney in California who has certain of his clients convey all of their property (both personal and business) and all rights to their small businesses to a CFC located in a tax haven. Thus, all income earned by the business goes to the CFC, as the owner.

The individual who used to own the business is then hired to work for the CFC as an employee, operating the business in its location in the United States, just as he/she would if it were owned by him/her. This individual is paid a small salary as an employee, *upon which taxes are paid*. The balance of the income of the business goes, formally, to the CFC.

The CFC itself is "run" by three nominee directors in the tax haven. According to the law of the tax haven, these nominees as the directors of the CFC have full power over the affairs of the CFC. In fact, the nominees take orders from the CFC's employees. (The tail wags the dog, in effect.) These directors, for example, pay out earnings to whomever the employee directs.

By now you have spotted the "catch" in this system. You remember the "attribution of ownership" rules. Since the "employee" is actually running the CFC, the income of the CFC is attributable and taxable to the employee, right?

Well, this would be the argument the IRS would make in court against the employee—*if the IRS could find the records* to support this argument. *But where are the records? In the tax haven.*

Can the IRS or any other government agency get those records? Does the subpoena power of the United States—the power to get records and testimony–extend beyond the jurisdiction of the U.S. courts? The answer, in the vast majority of cases, is "No." A treaty can allow this, of course, but a "tax haven" that would allow this would cease to be a tax haven, immediately.

The bottom line is, if the IRS can't get evidence as to the CFC, it has no case against the employee of the CFC. It is difficult to imagine the IRS proceeding against the employee without records, which are available only in the tax haven.

Now, bear in mind, *we are not advocating breaking the law.* We have stated the legal rules to you, and we think it is important for you to know them. However, the sort of arrangement just described happens frequently despite the rules. We are simply presenting this example as a part of the entire tax haven scene.

How A Professional Person May Benefit From Tax Havens

The question is sometimes asked whether there are advantages for the professional (lawyer, physician, architect, etc.) in using tax havens. The answer is a cautious "Yes." The flexibility on this matter stems from the same source as does flexibility on the matter of tax advantages domestically; namely, independence.

So what can the professional do to reduce his/her taxes by use of a tax haven?

By being an employee of a foreign corporation whose records are not available to the IRS by subpoena or otherwise, a professional can, in practical effect, even if not strictly in law, bar the prying eyes of the IRS from evidence showing his/her income.

The rules regarding "foreigners" (including foreign corporations) earning money in the U.S. are fairly strict. Performance of personal services within the U.S. constitutes "engaging in a U.S. trade of business." A non-resident alien or foreign corporation which is engaged in U.S. trade or business is taxed at U.S. rates on income from U.S. sources gained from the conduct of such trade or business. A foreigner engages in a U.S. trade of business if it does business through an *agent* (such as an employee). Section 864(b) (1) and (2) carves out a small exception:

"The term 'trade or business within the United States' includes the performance of personal services within the United States at any time within the taxable year, but does not include—

(1) Performance of personal services for foreign employer.

The performance of personal services—

(A) for a non-resident alien individual, foreign partnership, or foreign corporation, not engaged in trade or business within the United States, or (B) for an office or place of business maintained in a foreign country or in a possession of the United States by an individual who is a citizen or resident of the United States or by a domestic partnership or a domestic corporation, by a non-resident alien individual temporarily present in the United States for a period or periods not exceeding a total of 90 days during the taxable year and whose compensation for such services does not exceed in the aggregate $3,000.

So, aside from the practical "problem" of the IRS not being able to get at the records of a foreign corporation it cannot subpoena, upon what can the professional pin his/her hopes?

Well, you can make sure that the "business" you conduct occurs offshore. This would mean that a mailing address in the tax haven would be the chief point of contact between the professional and the client. (Convincing the IRS that services are being performed offshore may be difficult, of course.) In addition, all business correspondence should be sent out and received at the foreign address. Even so, if a non-resident alien individual or foreign corporation has U.S. source income "not effectively connected" with a U.S. trade or business, such U.S. source income is taxed at 30%, or at a lower rate if a treaty with a particular tax haven so provides.

Okay, so what if the professional takes "the ultimate step" and gives up U.S. citizenship, thus becoming an alien? This may be a way to reduce your income taxes, but only slightly. As made clear in the remainder of this book, the Internal Revenue Code does not leave an alien alone simply because of alien citizenship. Furthermore, if it is shown that one of the principal reasons why you gave up your U.S. citizenship was to avoid taxes, for *ten years* after your renunciation of U.S. citizenship you will be taxed at *regular U.S. rates* on U.S. source income and on income "effectively connected" to the conduct of a trade or business in the U.S.

2 What Tax Havens Are

A haven is a refuge from some kind of persecution. The persecution can be political, religious, social, economic, psychological, physical, or what have you. It can be against the person directly, or indirectly through his property. It can be in varying degrees of intensity; but by definition it is intense enough in the mind of the persecuted to send him seeking refuge.

A tax haven, therefore, is a refuge from tax persecution. Many individuals share the view that their earnings are their own property, and consequently are not a proper source of tax revenue. Other sources of revenue would be quite adequate, they maintain, if all the waste, inefficiency, duplication, and unjustified expenditures were eliminated from governmental operations. The disease is not peculiar to one nation or even a few. Persons in all parts of the world believe that the taxes imposed on them by their governments are unfair, excessive, and irresponsible. The very existence of tax havens is proof of the statement. For every problem there is a solution; for every demand, a supply. Tax havens are flourishing because frustrated taxpayers are patronizing them. Obviously, their patrons find this avenue of relief quicker, easier, and more productive for them than the alternative of trying to change the tax structure in their own country against entrenched public spending interests.

Tax havens in their initial stages of development provided the relief sought by a relatively small number of wealthy persons. It was they, after all, who were politically expendable. On a one-man-one-vote basis, their voting power totaled about three watts, even if they voted as a solid block. How logical, then, for a politician to aim at the mass vote market by promising government largesse to everyone except the wealthy, and designing the tax system to make the wealthy pay for it. Good strategy on paper, and for a long time it seemed that you could ". . . fool all the people all the time."

Water and economics, however, have a way of finding their own level. Even if all the wealthy persons paid all the taxes imposed on them by a discriminatory system, the total would be nowhere near enough money to pay the tax bills run up by the public spenders. Furthermore, the affluent citizens did what anyone else would do in the same situation: They invested money in political lobbying and campaigning to ease their burdens; and they went on a search for places outside their government's jurisdiction where they could deposit sums of their money with the blessings of other governments.

The significance of this maneuver is not the relatively few dollars kept away from the tax coffers. It goes much deeper than that. The real import lies in the feasibility of any tax system that causes the affluent persons in that system—the prime producers of the wealth on which every element of the system depends—to shun cooperation with the system and independently seek relief from its abuses. A law is only as effective as the support it receives from those on whom it is imposed. Our tax laws are becoming increasingly ineffective as they lose the support of the persons who produce the wealth and therefore the tax money.

The political efforts of the affluent did achieve substantial success, with the result that the theoretical top tax brackets became the actual middle and lower brackets. No one paid the top tax rate, or any percentage near it. And that is why the tax havens remained for many years a peculiarity used exclusively by small numbers of persons. Their only patrons were the very rich for whom legal loopholes at home were just partially adequate, or a few individuals who understandably chose anonymity in their financial affairs. The great mass of taxpayers avoided what they could and paid the remainder. They knew nothing about tax shelters and havens, nor even what the terms meant.

What has brought the subject increasingly to the attention of greater numbers of taxpayers is free economics, like water, seeking and finding its own level. Governments have a way of extracting money from those who have earned it and turning it over (minus the cost of counting it) to those who have not earned it. But the Robin Hood theory of taxation cannot work in dynamic society. It is self-defeating. Someone besides the wealthy few have to pay the bills that have been run up, and do it either through larger tax payments or higher inflation or both. We have now reached a stage in which the rising water is not just getting us wet—we are beginning to worry about being able to breathe. And our increasing worries about the safety of our equities is the growing demand that is producing a growing supply of safe places in which to tuck away some of the threatened equity.

Specifically, these are countries which have tax laws that are more lenient than the tax laws of countries from which the refugee capital comes. Admittedly, all of the world's tax havens did not design their tax policies to attract refugee capital. In most cases they happen to be small nations, or colonies of large nations, whose revenue demands are modest. Because they are physically small they are relatively unimportant in world politics, and therefore have largely escaped the machinations of social reformers and experimenters spawned by the larger industrial nations.

Some of them fare quite well with income only from import duties. Others tax their own citizens but not the income of non-residents whose enterprises earn income from outside sources. These countries are often stisfied with the fees they collect from the registration and annual license renewals of alien enterprises, along with the outside capital deposited in their banks. Yet even the taxes collected for business generated locally is unbelievably low in many of these countries, compared to what an enterprise would pay on the same income in the U.S., the U.K., Sweden, or other industrial nations.

Some of these tax-haven nations protest the label given to them; others openly welcome it. It must be noted here that tax collectors are more likely to scrutinize any business activities involving a well-publicized tax haven than they are if the country is not widely known as a tax haven. So to whatever extent their protests succeed in deflecting attention, to that extent are they more valuable to you, everything else being equal. Even those who resist their tax-haven reputation have to appreciate the infusion of outside capital into their domain. Certainly they could pass harsh laws to discourage foreign capital if they really wanted no part of it. At least one nation has, in fact, taken some steps in that direction; but by its exception among the traditional tax havens, it proves the rule. Switzerland, the haven of legend, has succeeded so well economically in recent years that she is having problems of a kind that do not bother the other members of the tax-haven fraternity. To strengthen her exports and tourist trade, she is penalizing foreign depositors and investors in an attempt to lower the value of her franc relative to other major currencies. Switzerland, in fact, gives the appearance of being downright anti-social with her tightening immigration laws, work visas, and other measures dealing with aliens. All this is almost academic to the subject of tax havens, actually, since there are other nations with all the advantages of Switzerland and more, and few if any of the handicaps.

For example, there are countries that do not tax individuals or companies on interest, dividends, salaries, appreciation of property or stock, inheritance, real estate, personal property, or purchases. Imagine what your present financial health would be if you could say that about your own country. Imagine the sense of freedom! Most of us, of course, work for other people; and unless we move to one of the tax paradises described and get a job at the same pay, we simply could not trade our present lot for the tax-free existence and realize any net gain in income. With all their tax burdens, Americans particularly enjoy higher salaries than their direct counterparts elsewhere, although the advantage is shrinking rapidly. Unless you would be satisfied solely with the psychological benefits of living tax-free, therefore, you will have to invest some capital in order to really benefit financially as well as psychologically. So when we talk about tax havens, we are necessarily talking about some form of investment, not about a physical relocation to escape taxes. For that matter, the laws of some so-called tax havens grant tax-free status *only* to foreign-based enterprise licensed there but earning profits elsewhere. The natives pay taxes, and so would you if you moved there and earned your livelihood there also.

This is not to say that you would not be a welcome visitor in any of these countries. All are hospitable, and for other reasons as well rate a visit or even temporary residence. The ones that collect no income taxes from anyone do, in fact, offer a very real incentive even to salaried Americans who would establish temporary residence and earn money for services performed outside the U.S. If you meet certain requirements (that we will go into later), you can exclude up to $15,000 income a year in most cases from U.S. taxes. Naturally you also have to meet the extended visa and other requirements of the country in which you are working. But what it all adds up to is a net income that is the same as your gross income during the time you are thus employed.

If you can't arrange to have your employer transfer you to the right foreign country, obviously you could set up your own U.S. corporationand transfer yourself wherever you wished. A point of caution, however: You can exclude from taxable income only 30 percent of your share of the income your company earns abroad, if you are a principal of the company, and if your income is substantially from capital growth rather than from your labor alone. That leads us right back to the point that you can avoid such limitations by establishing your enterprise as a foreign-based instead of a U.S.-based company. Then, regardless of how you take your compensation, you pay no taxes on it up to the $15,000* maximum—provided, of course, you have set it up in the right country.

The $15,000* exclusion for U.S. citizens employed abroad (see page 89 for further details) is just one angle of several that offer rewards to persons looking beyond their native shores for protection of their capital. For persons not willing to move outside the country, or who are interested in tax protection for more than $15,000* income, we come to the central premise of this book: establishing, at minimum cost to you, a company in one of the tax-haven countries covered in this book, and avoiding paying taxes on any of the income it generates.

Fine, you say, but which is the right country? The right one for you is the one that you decide is right, after reading the rest of this book and after getting confirmation and further details from the havens themselves. You might also want to discuss the options with a knowledgeable friend, tax lawyer, or accountant. If that sounds like buck-passing, it is not. It is only affirmation of what any prudent investor would do anyhow. The problem is that knowledgeable ad-

---

*This a general figure and may vary depending upon the circumstances.

vice in this field is very limited, and what there is, is very expensive. That is a point we have been repeating because it is the very reason this book was written. Middle-sized incomes need good, inexpensive, simplified advice on saving tax dollars the way the upper incomes do it.

You can get authoritative and inexpensive information on the politics, trade, transportation and banking facilities, business opportunities, and such other matters as would affect your enterprise. But inexpensive experts on the precise subject of tax havens are scarce if not nonexistent. If you happen to find someone who claims expertise on tax-haven matters, one purpose of this book is to make you sufficiently knowledgeable to judge their competence and objectivity. We do urge you to consult persons who have no preconceived negative notions about tax loopholes and havens.

As we said, the designation of any country as a tax haven is an arbitrary matter, inasmuch as the term has no official sanction. No country qualifies by meeting some authorized set of standards. There is no international league of tax havens, except tacitly through the sharing of common policies and attributes. It is their policies of benevolence toward individual rights, private property, including capital and its owners' right to benefit from its appreciation; it is their attributes of modern communications and travel facilities, of economic substance, strong modern banks, and political stability— these policies and attributes that qualify them as tax havens. As you measure the relative presence of these features in each haven, and such additional considerations as language, proximity, and currency controls, your final choice or choices will depend on the best combination of policies and attributes for you.

Shopping for a house mortgage offers a good example of what we mean. One bank offers the lowest interest rate but requires a larger down payment. Another bank will finance a larger amount of the market price, but at a higher interest rate. A third bank charges less interest but requires a shorter term and therefore higher monthly payments. In still another bank you find a good rate, term, and per cent of financing, but also a substantial prepayment penalty. Obviously, if the only choice you had to make was interest rate, you would simply pick the bank with the lowest rate. But you almost never find an apples-to-apples comparison in the same market. So you have to decide, after considering all the features of every bank in your area, which one suits you and your circumstances best. And that's how it is with tax havens.

Just as you would make a list of the banks and their mortgage features, so that later you could compare them and make a decision, so with tax havens we have made a list of the ones we believe deserve your consideration, and include a brief commentary on each. Then at the end of the listing you will find a chart that lays them all out with their respective features for graphic comparison. If you agree with the author's conclusions favoring two particular havens over the others, you will find the starting of a company or a trust in one of those havens quite simple. It will be as simple as filling out the forms in this book and dropping them in the mail along with the necessary fees.

First, however, we need to discuss the reasons for mentioning certain features besides the taxing policies and practices of each haven. Once again, some of these features will be academic to you for your purposes, but highly important to some one else for his own reasons.

Transportation: Airports, seaports, capacities, and schedules are vital, irrelevant, or somewhere in between, depending on whether all your business will be in volume commerce, or conducted casually through occasional correspondence with the bank or agent representing you, or managed by you (and perhaps partners) actively and from positions both local and remote. If you are receiving raw materials and shipping manufactured goods, you will obviously rely on air, land, and sea shipping facilities. (Such an operation suggests an enterprise that might be beyond the scope and intent of this book.) If your enterprise is organizing and running business meetings, you will need air service with major cities as well as recreational transportation and all the other requirements of a business meeting. But if your investment is in a business that sells mail-order products or books you write now and then, is in a trust for your children, or in a small investment business, then once-a-week mail delivery would be more than ample.

Proximity: Frequent travel and/or communication with your tax haven obviously will cost less if the distance between is relatively short. Otherwise, distance is hardly a problem for business conducted by letter, unless it poses a psychological problem. Proximity to markets and supply sources would be very important also for a multinational manufacturing company. This book, however, is not written for such an enterprise unless it happens to operate on a very modest scale.

Communications: The same considerations apply here as with transportation. How often and how quickly will you have to communicate between your residence, your business, and perhaps other foreign locations? You have to remember that several good tax havens are small and fairly remote. They might consist of several islands, with the principal island connected to the mainland by telephone and wire cables, but to its satellite islands only by radio telephone. Instantaneous teletype and digital wire service might not be available at all. Remember too that keeping current with local and world affairs while visiting your haven will call for first-class television, radio, newspaper, and magazine service, which in turn depend on transportation, telephone, wire, and cable facilities.

Language: If your mother tongue is English you will have a minimum of problems, and in most of the countries listed, no trouble at all. Not only is English the native, or at least the government and commercial language of perhaps half of those listed, it is spoken as a second language in most of the others. Spanish, German, and French are also prominent among tax-haven countries. If a country rates as a recommended tax haven otherwise, language will be a mild inconvenience at worst.

Professional Services: These include legal, accounting, banking, insurance, engineering realty, and perhaps others such as medical, architectural, and so forth. What help you will need will be determined by the nature of your involvement from a personal as well as a business standpoint. If your enterprise is entirely or mainly on paper, your needs will be limited to legal, banking, insurance, and accounting, along with clerical and perhaps agency assistance. You can, in fact, hire the services of an agent who will represent your interests in every regard. Even though you could get extensive help from your chosen bank, from the embassy representing the tax-haven nation in your own country, and even from your own consulate in that nation, none of these provide the convenience if indeed even the capability of an experienced agent. After all, handling all the investment details for persons like you is his business! You would, of course, select him with the same care you would exercise in choosing any other delegate of such consequence: Check his other clients (although some agents might rightfully not reveal clients' identities), his references, your own references. If you do not use them otherwise, here is where the embassies, consulates, banks, chambers of commerce and better business bureaus, trade associations, professional societies, and others can aid you. A polite request by letter will get a helpful reply from any of these sources. Their counterparts in your own country can provide you with names and addresses. As a starting point, this book will give you names and addresses of agents in the favored tax havens, and you can then proceed to check them out through your local bank or other source suggested.

Currency and Exchange Control: Some nations are pretty strict about letting their currency out of the country. Non-resident corporations have to get permission to exchange their foreign currency for local money to conduct any local transactions; and conversely, any resident corporation needs permission to convert local money to foreign currency for transactions outside that country. At the same time, however, a non-resident corporation such as you would be operating is usually free to bring in any amount of foreign money and send out any amount, as long as it is associated entirely with business outside that country (and provided you meet any requirements of the sending and receiving countries). Some of the countries listed have those same requirements written in their codes but do not exercise them. And at least half of the better tax havens exercise no controls whatever.

Political and Economic Stability: Needless to say, you will not want to entrust your investment to any nation that has a recent history of revolution or violent threats of it. Nor should you consider any country whose future stability is in serious question. There are many new nations in the world, and some of them are trying to entice foreign investment by calling themselves tax havens. We will recommend them, perhaps, at some later date after they have proved themselves worthy of confidence. We will never recommend a nation that embraces a politico-economical ideology that is basically antithetical to the ideals of individual rights, private property, capitalism, and free enterprise. We will not, for example, recommend Zaire, formerly the Belgian Congo, or Hungary. Zaire has a recent violent past and revolution in government as well as an uncertain future. Hungary is a puppet of the Kremlin, and we know too well what they think of private property, profits, and promises. It amazes us that those two (and some others) even suggest that private investors should consider them. Finally, there are several countries whose hearts are in the right place but who for various economic reasons do not in our estimation merit serious consideration by the readers of this book.

3 Where The Tax Havens Are

As we said earlier, a few countries do not like to be called tax havens. But if the shoe fits, they wear it. One also hears arguments by some haven-watchers that this or that country referred to as a tax haven does not deserve the term, or that other countries are illogically excluded. We are not here to debate what constitutes the perfect list. We are here to look at any and all countries that might provide shelter for the assets of a nation's producers against its non-producers who would take their assets away from them. The term "producers" encompasses the industrial nations' large middle class of small businessmen, salaried and wage-roll employees. We therefore limit our considerations to the tax havens and to the kinds of investment that would be appropriate for that group. The comments for each country are made accordingly.

Andorra

This is a tiny country tucked away in the Pyrenees Mountains between France and Spain. It offers a quaint mixture of both cultures and its own, of the antique and modern. Its population enjoys a high standard of living, largely because of an almost total absence of taxes and an abundance of bargains in the marketplace. Because its government has closed the door to the formation of non-resident companies, our only point in mentioning it is its attractiveness as a residential tax haven. If you are ready to pull up stakes, liquidate all your assets and take them with you out of the country, Andorra could provide the Good Life for you on a modest income. Your dwindling purchasing power and relative earning capacity can be turned around in a country that has no income taxes on corporations or individuals, no capital gains tax, no estate or inheritance taxes, or customs duties. You probably would be able to afford periodic visits to your home country, where you could also enjoy the continuing benefits of citizenship.

Antigua

Antigua is one of the easternmost islands of the Caribbean, a self-governing Associated State with Britain. With its sister state-islands of Barbados, Grenada, and St. Vincent, Antigua provides certain benefits that make it worth looking at as a tax haven. Besides charging no tax on income or dividends of foreign *non-investment* companies based there but operating outside, and a 2.5 per cent tax on the *net* income received by the same kind of *investment* companies, Antigua qualifies such companies for treaty benefits between the U.S. and the U.K. Specifically, your tax on dividend received from your Antigua-based company could be reduced from 30 per cent to about 17 per cent as a perfectly legal result of that treaty.

Bahamas

Since 1973 an independent nation within the British Commonwealth, this near-neighbor of the United States is one of the leading tax havens in the world, with probably 13,000 companies based there. Although its population is less than 200,000—about half in Nassau, the rest scattered over many of its 700 island—it boasts completely modern facilities and is host each year to a million tourists, who constitute the Bahamas' main source of income. It has no income taxes, no corporate taxes, no capital gains or withholding taxes on dividends and interest paid, and no estate taxes. New Providence Island, which contains Nassau, taxes improved real estate properties; but the Freeport area on Grand Bahama Island guarantees to licensed companies no taxes—including real estate taxes—until at least 1990, and no commercial import or stamp duties until the year 2054. If you are contemplating a business that involves importing goods into the Bahamas, you will need an import license. And, as in any tax haven, you will have to pay a filing fee and an annual registration fee for any kind of company. The total cost of incorporation might run $1,100 with annual fees and other management and clerical expenses totaling about $500 for a small company.

Barbados

A fully independent nation within the British Commonwealth, it offers essentially the same benefits to the foreign investor as its neighbors in the eastern Caribbean—Antigua, Grenada, St. Vincent, Montserrat, and British Virgin Islands. There are specific differences among them, but mainly they are differences of degree rather than of kind. For example, they all enjoy treaty benefits with the U.S. which reduce the tax rate on dividends of U.S. corporations paid to shareholder companies licensed in any of these countries. The rate varies from 2 per cent in St. Vincent up to 20 per cent in Montserrat, which is still substantially below the 30 per cent one would have to pay without the treaty (15 per cent paid to U.S. credited against Montserrat 20 per cent tax, plus the 5 per cent difference owed Montserrat). The low 2 per cent rate in St. Vincent does not appear to be as sound a deal as the 2.5 per cent in Barbados, since St. Vincent's banking system is of dubious stability (with no banking legislation, any company can operate as a bank), while Barbados provides first-class banking and other facilities. Furthermore, if your company is not an investment company, it pays no taxes at all in Barbados. At the same time, however, it does not qualify for the U.S. treaty benefits, as does an investment company that pays the 2.5 per cent tax.

None of the aforementioned countries is as convenient to the United States as the Bahamas, Bermuda, or the Cayman Islands. There is good jet service, particularly to Barbados, but it still takes four times as long to get there. English is the language of all these countries, ranging from the cultured British accent of Nassau (spoken also by the black majority) to a heavy Caribbean accent spoken by the preponderantly black native populations of Barbados and the other islands of eastern Caribbean.

One other possible disadvantage to incorporating in Barbados besides distance is death duty of 30 to 40 per cent taken from the shares of non-resident owners when they die. One way to avoid this death duty is to have the Barbadian corporation owned by a foreign corporation or trust rather than by individuals. Alternatively, your Barbadian company does not have to be incorporated in Barbados. It can be incorporated, for example, in the Cayman Islands and licensed to conduct business in Barbados. Then you would pay no death duty to Barbados or the Cayman. That way, too, you might enjoy the no-tax freedom of Cayman at the same time you benefit from the tax treaty between Barbados and the United States, a treaty that is not available to no-tax havens such as the Cayman Islands.

Finally on the negative side is the requirement by Barbados (and Antigua, Grenada, St. Vincent, Montserrat, and B.V.I.) that every company file an income-tax return, whether tax is owed or not. The drudgery of paper work is not the main problem here, but the mere presence of a document detailing one's earnings. Fortunately, as an official policy, this information as well as one's regular banking activities is held in strictest confidence and will not be disclosed to any outside source, including foreign revenue agents. That does not provide iron-clad protection against a determined inquiry, which would probably occur, however, only if the taxing jurisdiction got wind of very large profits or serious criminal acts. Furthermore, many companies register with nominee directors who are native to the tax-haven country. Even though they are dummy directors, the practice is quite legal and it protects the anonymity of the real directors and with it, their peace-of-mind. Still, such protection for individuals and corporations cannot be so strong in any tax haven having treaties with nations claiming tax rights to their incomes as the protection afforded by havens not bound by such treaties. So once again we say that a given tax haven is right or wrong for an individual depending on what he wants to do with his money. No single haven is best in all respects for any type of investment.

Bermuda

For Americans, no tax haven is closer or more convenient than Bermuda. In other important respects too it looks like a prime choice for Americans and Canadians hotly pursued by the tax collectors. There are no taxes. Facilities are first-rate. English is the language.

A closer examination, however, reveals possible deterrents to the general run of middle-income investors. Bermuda is rather snobbish about who organizes a business in their fair country. An Advisory Committee appointed by the Minister of Finance passes on all applications, and only persons with the best bank references and personal credentials are allowed to organize in Bermuda. Furthermore, incorporation and annual fees are higher than many other havens, and companies must issue shares amounting to at least $12,000. It isn't even a good retirement location for anyone wanting to own his retirement residence. Bermuda is very stingy about alien ownership of property, a factor largely of its very limited geography.

British Virgin Islands

This is a small British Crown Colony in the Caribbean located near the American islands of St. Thomas, St. John, and St. Croix. B.V.I. has close economic and social ties with the American islands and, in fact, uses the U.S. dollar as its official currency. Recognizing the problems posed by its small (10,000 population) size, it is openly boosting its status as a tax haven, although it prefers the term "financial center." As mentioned in the references to Antigua and Barbados, B.V.I. offers the advantages (and disadvantages) of tax treaties with the U.S. and other nations. This cuts in half the tax paid by B.V.I. companies on dividends received from U.S. corporations, for example, although it has no effect on interest received from U.S. sources. The government is encouraging tourism development, but any income from such investment pays a flat 12 per cent tax. That is low compared to your experience, but is high compared to some other countries.

Cayman Islands

This British Crown Colony consists of three islands and a population of about 16,000, of which one-fifth is white, one-fifth black, and the remainder mixed. They all speak English. If there is a tax paradise anywhere in the world, this must be it. To put it simply, there are not taxes of any kind. The modest costs of government are borne comfortably by import duties, stamp duties on most documents, and fees on businesses. Technically, these forms of revenue could be called taxes, but they are negligible compared with anything else called a tax imposed by other countries. As for taxes on any kind or amount of income, it is possible even to acquire a government guarantee against any taxes for a specified number of years (20 for companies, 50 for trusts) in the future. The safeguarding of proprietary information is as near absolute as anywhere else in the world, with the divulging of any kind of information to outside sources punishable under the law. The identity of beneficial shareholders is not required, nor is any financial declaration. One might question the professional and technical capabilities of a sovereignty so small, but the recent influx of investment attracted from other havens attests to its modern company and trust laws, the excellence of its banking, legal, and other services, and the proficiency of its transportation and communications facilities. For the reasons mentioned, as well as for others that deserve further discussion, we will deal with the Cayman Islands at greater length in Chapter Eight.

Channel Islands

Located in the English Channel, closer to France than to England, these autonomous possessions of the British Crown enjoy the protection and resources of Britain along with almost complete freedom in local government. Each of the four—Jersey, Guernsey, Alderney, and Sark—has its own laws, court system, governing body and local customs, evolved over the centuries through ancient charters and adaptations of English common law with occasional overlays of French law. Some legal terms and contracts, in fact, are written in French, and some of the natives speak a French patois along with the standard English.

Because these islands are some of the last remnants of the once world-wide Sterling Area, they serve as tax havens primarily for British business. But while their Sterling Area status allows the free flow of currency between the Channel Islands and United Kingdom financial centers, it also hinders the flow of currency between the

Islands and countries outside the Sterling Area. For the heavily-taxed British, the 20 per cent levied by the Islands against local income and the 300 pounds (about $558) charged companies earning external income, represent substantial tax savings. Sark charges no income tax at all, although its resources cannot support extensive outside business involvement. Otherwise, there are no capital gains taxes, no estate duties, no gift taxes, and no death duties.

Gibraltar

This is another British Crown Colony, one that is only about two square miles in area and inhabited by 25,000 English-speaking citizens, mostly of British extraction. It is a member of the Sterling Area, so its currency is the Gibraltar pound sterling, freely exchangeable with the British pound. Local companies pay 37.5 per cent income tax, but non-resident companies conducting business outside Gibraltar qualify for exempt status and pay no tax. They can also deal freely in non-sterling currency (but not in sterling). Indeed, their share capital must be expressed in a currency other than sterling (or the Swiss franc). Their exempt status also guarantees them freedom from income tax for 25 years. No Gibraltar company pays a capital gains tax and no exempt company pays death or estate duties at the death of its owner or beneficiary shareholders. There is no sales tax either, but documents involved in the transfer of property require stamps costing a maximum of 1.25 per cent of the sale.

One of the biggest drawbacks to the establishment of a business in Gibraltar is its dispute with Spain. Despite the almost total desire of Gibraltarians to remain British, Spain has been exerting strong pressure to win control, and has closed all land communications with Gibraltar as one move in its campaign. As a result, Gibraltar relies entirely on air and sea transportation, which are excellent, and certainly suffers no more than many an island nation in this respect. The only serious aspect of this development is the political cloud injected as a negative variable with which other tax havens do not have to contend.

Hong Kong

You might have noticed that a lot of business and commerce emanate from this British Crown Colony. It might also seem peculiar that this geographically small, almost totally Chinese state should be in the main-stream of international business affairs. Indeed it is a leading business center, second only to Tokyo in the Far East. The reasons for its success are manifold, but not least among them have been the strong influence of British law, business know-how, and political stability. Even though 98 per cent of its four million population are Chinese who speak Chinese to each other, the official language is English, and all government and business agents speak English. Another important factor supporting its growth has been its tax structure, which imposes low taxes on local activities and virtually none on business entities registered in Hong Kong but earning income elsewhere. Add to these reasons the modern transportation, communications and professional facilities of Hong Kong, and you begin to understand why it has attracted so much capital. In fact, Hong Kong enjoys perhaps unparalleled benefits from the reciprocity between its business and its tax policies: Business is drawn there by the absence of or the low taxes; and tax-refugee capital is attracted by the strong commercial environment and reputation that tend to obscure the purely tax-haven activities in its midst.

Because of its unique status as the country with the best balance between its commercial and tax-haven features, we are saving Hong Kong along with the Cayman Islands for extensive review in Chapter Eight.

Isle of Man

This Irish Sea island with the intriguing name is one of the British Isles but is not a part of the United Kingdom. It enjoys much the same status as the Channel Islands discussed earlier, and would be grouped with them for simplicity of discussion,except that geographically it is quite separate from them and culturally somewhat different also. Like the others, it relies on Great Britain for defense and foreign affairs, but otherwse is self-governing. Its tax laws are similar to those of Jersey and Guernsey, resident companies and individuals paying 21.25 per cent income tax; but a Manx company that is controlled from another country is exempt from income taxes. (Manx—a Manx company—is the adjective for Isle of Man, and is most often used in reference to the island's famous breed of tail-less cat). No company or individual pays a capital gains tax, a wealth tax, an estate, inheritance, or gift tax. They do limit interest rates to a maximum of 10 per cent a year. Obviously, with its relatively few taxes, its easy accessibility from Britian and Ireland, and its membership in the Sterling Area, it is principally of benefit to British and Irish businessmen. On net balance, other tax havens offer more to Americans and other nationalities shopping for tax havens.

Liberia

The only tax haven in Africa, this nation on the west coast of Africa, eight and one half hours by air from New York, was formed in 1847 by freed American slaves with extensive assistance from the U.S. The American influence is strong, which makes Liberia especially interesting to U.S. citizens. Its constitution and government are patterned after those of the U.S.; its legal tender is the U.S. dollar; its official language is English; and its corporation laws are almost the same as Delaware corporation laws—the most familiar (and most friendly to business) of the fifty States.

Furthermore, Liberia has learned what most other nations have failed (or refused) to learn: how to simplify and streamline government to minimize bureaucratic red tape. This phenomenon, coupled with stability of government and modern business facilities, has attracted investment capital from all parts of the world. This is particularly true for shipping enterprises. Liberia, a nation of only 1,200,000, has more shipping tonnage registered than any other nation in the world—three times as much as the U.S., in fact.

For anyone considering Liberia as a tax haven, the pros far outweigh the cons. Taxes for local enterprise are low, and for companies and trusts externally owned and receiving all income from outside sources, there are no taxes. Perhaps even more important, private companies do not have to report financial matters or director changes. Companies may issue bearer shares (freely transferable like cash), par value shares, or shares with no par value. Annual stockholder meetings can be held anywhere in the world. There is no exchange control, so one can deal in any currencies that are convenient.

There are rules, of course, but quite reasonable ones. You must, for example, put up at least $500 capital to register a company; and you have to pay annual fees of $100. Other than maintaining a resident business agent (provided by a Liberian trust), there is no need for the physical presence in Liberia of any company representative at any time. Nominee directors will be provided by the Liberian trust company at no extra charge, and a Liberian trust even maintains offices in New York and Zurich to handle all the details of incorporation at no cost.

One of Liberia's few drawbacks is its location. It is in a strategic location for shipping, but there are good tax havens nearer than Liberia to any of the high-tax industrial nations. Unless you want to or have to visit your tax haven, however, the distance is no problem. Transportation and communication facilities are first-rate. Other possible detractions are its physical and social attributes. It gets a lot of rain, has a long rainy season, and is humid all the time. The so-called "civilized" population—English-speaking, educated, Protestant—that runs the government and business is a minority, numbering fewer than one-tenth of the population. The remainder is divided among twenty-odd tribes. There are probably a thousand white residents, but the law requires black African heritage for citizenship.

Liechtenstein

Many persons really think that Liechtenstein is a fairy-tale country. It is a real country all right and has been for a very long time. The relatively few tourists who manage to get there, nevertheless, still find a fairy-tale country. Because of its isolation in the mountains between Switzerland and Austria, it hasn't changed much over the centuries. And because of its small population and geography, it hasn't received much attention. That is perhaps the main reason why many persons, particularly many Europeans, for many years have put their money there.

Ironically, however, its very attractiveness as a sanctuary and its success in attracting outside wealth, in recent years have begun to result in a reverse effect. Even though industry has been growing in the past several decades, its main industry is still in the registration of outside financial interests. In fact, the estimated 20,000 nonresident business entities registered in the country about equal the total population. Its world-wide reputation as a tax haven is therefore causing apprehension in some circles as authorities in tax-heavy nations bore in on individuals discovered to have connections with Liechtenstein-domiciled enterprises.

That is not to suggest, however, any general calamity for the principals of these enterprises or for those who set up a company or trust there in the future. Liechtenstein protects financial privacy at least as strictly as Switzerland, whose currency and banking facilities she uses. Violations are punishable under the law. Liechtenstein has only one tax treaty, and that one, with Austria, might soon be abolished; so the required trading of tax information with other countries is not a problem. On the other hand, the laws do require a more detailed reporting of activities than other tax havens require.

A so-called domiciliary company, which is one domiciled or registered there but doing business only outside the country, is exempt from taxes on property, earnings, and profits, but must pay a capital tax at one-tenth per cent of total invested capital, with a minimum of 1,000 francs a year (about $400). It also pays a 3 per cent coupon tax on distributed dividends. A holding company is subject to the same taxes. There are no exchange controls.

Liechtenstein has two investment entities that are unusual if not unique. One is the *stiftung*, or foundation, but a foundation designed entirely or partly to benefit a family. The other is the *anstalt*, translated "establishment," but with its own special meaning. In many ways the *foundation* is like a discretionary trust. It must be endowed with a minimum of 30,000 francs (about $12,000), and it can receive donations from any source. It is administered by an appointed board, acting under the founding articles. The *establishment* can have one founder, who is the supreme authority. It must have at least one director, who can be the founder, but must have a director domiciled in Liechtenstein. (This could be a nominee, or titular director.) Like the company, the foundation, and the trust, the establishment must have a minimum capital of 30,000 francs. It pays a formation duty of 2 per cent of its capital, minimum 600 francs ($240), and also one-tenth per cent a year on total capital, minimum 1,000 francs ($400).

Countries operating under civil law do not ordinarily provide the opportunity for setting up a trust that common-law countries do, and Liechtenstein operates essentially under Austrian civil law. Even so, there are many trusts established here, and of quite a variety. There are family foundation types, business trusts, and trusts acting as holding companies. One reason for having a business trust instead of a company is that the trust does not have to be listed in the Public Register. But it pays the same taxes as the other enterprises.

For an American, or even a Briton, this would be less attractive a tax haven than several others. The language is German, although government and business activities can be conducted in English. There is no commercial airport, the closest being Zurich, two hours away by train, and the train doesn't even stop at Vaduz, the capital; you have to take a bus from the nearest station. These inconveniences might even be an asset if they also meant that tax collectors the world over were not scrutinizing the place, which they are (without results in most cases). But why risk harrassment, even if one is entirely legal? Since there is no equivalent to the *anstalt* or *stiftung* in other countries, the home-country tax authorities could be quite arbitrary in their interpretation of any case involving these two entities.

Luxembourg

We are including Luxembourg, even though it is of very limited value as a tax haven, because one element has attracted a lot of attention in the financial community and should be mentioned. We are speaking of holding companies. If a holding company becomes important in your financial planning, then Luxembourg (and perhaps the Netherlands) should be looked at more closely. Actually, the fame of Luxembourg holding companies might be due mainly to a comparison of their tax status with that of other kinds of enterprise. In a nation that applies tax rates as high as 50 per cent, any entity enjoying nearly tax-free income is bound to look good. There are annual expenses beyond the initial costs, consisting primarily of .16

per cent on the value of debentures (debts owed to the company) and of issued shares, plus the cost of publishing a yearly financial statement. There's not much that is private about doing business in or through Luxembourg. Annual stockholder meetings have to be advertised and must be held in Luxembourg (although proxies are accepted); financial statements must be filed quarterly and published in the official journal; and tax treaties with numerous other nations guarantee the broad dissemination of information, if requested, without providing any double taxation benefits to holding companies, small though they might be if the .16 per cent were credited.

So even though Luxembourg boasts some of the best in transportation and communications facilities, economic and political stability, we do not see much benefit in it as a tax haven. Moreover, judging from recent threatening sounds from the EEC (European Economic Community, better known as the European Common Market), of which it is a member, even the holding company benefit might be nullified in a few years.

Monaco

Looked at objectively, there is not much to recommend Monaco as a tax haven. But if for some reason it has caught your fancy, there are several points worth mentioning besides its romantic atmosphere. First of all, everyone living in Monaco is free from income tax except French citizens. The discrimination against the French was Charles de Gaulle's, not Prince Rainier's. President de Gaulle was incensed by the outrageous and substantial emigration of Frenchmen for the unpatriotic reason of avoiding income taxes, and he leaned hard on Monaco for a new tax treaty, which was signed in 1963. Unlike other tax havens, which exempt non-resident companies earning money outside the country, Monaco taxes companies earning more than 25 per cent of their business outside the principality. If, however, your company is organized outside Monaco but maintains administrative offices there, you would pay only 35 per cent tax on 8 per cent of your office expenses. If the expenses were $10,000 a year, your tax would be about $280.

Montserrat

We have already largely covered this British Crown Colony in the preceeding sections on Antigua, Barbados, Grenada, St. Vincent, and British Virgin Islands. Even though Montserrat offers basically the same benefits as its Caribbean neighbors, it is smaller than the others, less accessible, and has higher taxes.

The Netherlands

Despite its very high taxes, the Netherlands deserve a brief word of commendation for its refusal to double-tax income. Holding companies registered there pay no tax on dividends received from business-related affiliates subject to dividend tax by another country, whether taxes were paid on the dividends or not. Netherlands' companies paying dividends are taxed at 25 per cent, unless one of the many tax treaties the Dutch have with other nations reduces or eliminates the tax. There is no withholding tax on interest.

As for regular companies, taxes are about as high as anywhere else in the world. The Dutch have tried to help business keep some of its financial matters private by creating a new kind of corporation and allowing companies to convert from the old type to the new. This circumvents some of the Common Market's directives requiring publication of detailed financial information by businesses in the member nations. Nevertheless, the long range outlook for tax advantages anywhere in the EEC is grim, and so we cannot recommend any of them as a refuge from taxes.

Netherlands Antilles

Formerly the Dutch West Indies, this autonomous territory of the Kingdom of the Netherlands consists of six islands, the most important of which are Curacao and Aruba. Besides a local native language, the people speak Dutch, English, and Spanish.

Despite the absence of capital gains tax, sales tax, or withholding taxes on dividends or interest paid to its non-resident shareholders, regular corporations here pay income taxes that are almost as high as in the U.S. So we will save your time talking about them except to mention that, if you are interested in manufacturing, there are Free Zone areas in Curacao and Aruba that eliminate duties and cut taxes by two-thirds. Probably the only areas of interest to the small, first-time user of a tax haven are investment or holding companies. These pay only a tenth of the income taxes paid by regular corporations, or less than 3 per cent. In the treaties the Netherlands Antilles has with the U.S., the U.K., Holland, Surinam, Denmark, and Norway, special provisions also favor these entities, along with regular companies.

Actually, it is the U.S. treaty that has given this haven a unique status. Under the treaty, dividends from U.S. sources are taxed by the U.S. at 15 per cent of the gross and by the Netherlands Antilles at 15 per cent net on the remaining 85 per cent. This is admittedly lower than the straight 30 per cent of gross a corporation would pay the U.S. without the treaty, but it certainly is no bargain. Interest and royalties income from U.S. sources are exempt from U.S. tax as long as they are taxed in the Antilles at the standard 24 per cent of net. This is a feature that Barbados, with its lower tax on U.S. dividends, does not provide.

Gains from the sale of securities, short- or long-term, are exempt from both U.S. and Antilles tax.

Perhaps the activity for which the Netherlands Antilles is best known, because of widespread participation in it, is the investment in U.S. real estate by holding companies registered there. A nonresident holding company pays no tax to the N.A. government on income from U.S. real estate, but does pay the U.S. tax. It also pays 2.4 per cent, plus a municipal surtax of 15 per cent on real estate capital gains. If the company earns income from property in Holland or Surinam (also Dutch), it pays no tax at all. If it earns money from real estate in any other country, the company pays the Antilles taxes of 2.4 and 15 per cent plus the tax to the other country. Or the company can elect to waive capital losses and depreciation deductions in favor of paying no surtax or capital gains tax.

New Hebrides

For the businessman longing to move his operations far far away from the clutches of home-country revenue offices and paper-proliferating bureaucracy, this is about as far as he can get. That is, unless he is an Australian, New Zealander, or other citizen of the Pacific Basin. New Hebrides is an island cluster located at almost the diametric opposite side of the globe from London and almost a full day of travel and layover time from the United States. Even Australia is 1,200 miles away (southwest) at its closest airport. So New Hebrides is remote.

And it is peculiar in its government arrangement. The eighty-odd thousand Melanesian natives govern themselves through local councils and native courts and have no real central authority. The five thousand or so residents of European extraction are governed by either a French authority or a British, depending on your national origin. If neither French nor British, you take your pick and abide thenceforth by that government. The two cultures stick pretty much to themselves speaking their respective languages, attending their own schools, generally shopping in their French or their British stores, and spending either Australian dollars or New Hebrides francs. The Australian dollar, worth about U.S. $1.30, is the primary currency, since most businesses are British. About the only shared activity is the Joint Court, the highest appellate court in the country. It consists of three judges, with the majority alternating between the British and the French.

Despite its isolation, New Hebrides has all the modern appurtenances to handle the most sophisticated businesses: banks, trust companies, legal and accounting firms, air service, and communications. The latter are at present the weakest point in the line-up, especially the radio-telephone service. Telex has its problems too, but cables are very reliable, and all facilities are improving steadily. Mail from the U.S. takes about a week.

Since you are wondering why we even mention such a distant and difficult place to get to, we must first reiterate that there is no need ever to take your person to your tax haven. You can run your business with perfect ease and assurance by mail, wire, cable, and telephone. We would not recommend the New Hebrides for fast-action business such as trading in futures, commodities, stock speculations, and other activities that depend on close timing and maximum communication. After all, New Hebrides offices are never open at the same time as offices in the world's major financial centers. But many readers of this book are not interested in that kind of business anyhow.

The biggest thing going for you in New Hebrides besides the absence of taxes (repeat, *no* taxes if you don't consider small annual fees of tax), is *secrecy*. The government—or governments—here protect your business privacy with laws. You do have to clearly identify your beneficiary shareholders to the government, and you have to file an annual, audited tax return. But these matters are held in strictest confidence. Furthermore. New Hebrides has no tax treaties with other countries and therefore no exchange of financial information. This, and several of the other tax havens covered in this book, come about as close to an absolute guarantee of privacy as you can get. In fact, New Hebrides is one of the last places in the world a tax collector would go hunting, which makes it most attractive for persons interested in being left alone by governments.

This does not include shady characters without impeccable references. Every application must contain the full name (no initials) and home address of every beneficiary shareholder, along with bank and other references. The New Hebrides government puts the screening responsibility on the trust company, bank, or law firm handling the organization but spot checks new companies as an added security against undesirable elements. Continuing control over unwanted activities resides in the local nominee director or directors of a company, who participate more actively in its affairs than do nominee directors elsewhere. This might sound like too much snooping, but in practice there is little involvement by the local agents once they are satisfied that a company or trust is legitimate.

Panama

Many persons, especially Americans, think of Panama as consisting only of the Canal and the Canal Zone. Even though geographically located in the nation of Panama, the Canal Zone is a minor entity, measured both by its population and the real estate it occupies. From a business standpoint, it is a nonentity: Its only residents are American military and naval personnel and families, civilians employed directly in the operation of the Canal and supporting facilities; and the supporting facilities are the only businesses as such located within the Canal Zone.

As for the nation of Panama, here is one of the major entities of the world for business and commerce. Largely because of its crossroads location, it is a sea, air, and land transportation center; and because of its location also, large and small companies of many kinds and many countries have established themselves in Panama, along with all the ancillary enterprises required by business. These include branches of the biggest names in banks and accounting firms from the U.S. and Europe. Panamanian banks, accountants, and attorneys are numerous and first-rate also. And there are many management firms that handle any or all business details for their clients. Altogether, one can say that the environment is very favorable for business, especially for business that earns its income from sources outside the country.

Companies that earn income from sources in Panama pay substantial taxes; other companies pay none. And that fact, along with the other benefits mentioned, is the reason why more than 35 thousand foreign companies—more than all other tax havens in the Western Hemisphere combined—have registered there. Other advantages include freely exchangeable currency (Panama coins and U.S. coins and currency have equal value and are both legal tender), no tax treaties with other countries, and protection of privacy.

Registration is relatively fast, easy, and inexpensive. The law requires two incorporators, three directors, a president, secretary, and treasurer for the formation of a corporation. Since the law allows one person to handle two or more jobs, three persons can form a corporation, as long as the job of secretary is not assumed by the same director who is president. The two persons who execute the articles of incorporation before a Panama notary can be nominees provided by your agent there and so can the three directors and officers. The more nominees you have, of course, the higher will be your annual costs, since you have to pay each a fee of perhaps $200 a year. Because directors can be of any nationality, the only reason for retaining more than the one Panama lawyer required as resident agent would be relative anonymity. (As we have said, there is no such thing as absolute legal anonymity in transactions involving any country. Privacy depends on the number of persons in the haven who know your identity and on what their laws do or do not require of them.) Panama, by the way, will provide numbered bank accounts the same as Switzerland and a number of other countries.

Panama does not require fully paid-up capital, although you do have to state the authorized capital of your company. The incorporation fee, called a Capital Stock Tax, is determined by the level of capitalization, with minimum of $20. Shares may or may not have a stated par value; they can be nominative or bearer type, common or preferred, voting or non-voting. Other features of the incorporation are the standard requirements of the corporation's name, its objects, its duration, domicile, names and addresses of directors (either nominee or beneficiary), and of the resident agent. The agent does not have to file reports with the Panama Government, but a bound minute book and stock register book must be maintained for examination by a local court judge. Altogether, a small corporation might cost about $600 to get started.

A very prominent feature of the Panama business scene is the Canal Free Zone, an industrial area at the Caribbean end of the Canal. Companies located here need no commercial license and pay no duties. If their purchases and sales involve no movement of goods through Panama, they pay no taxes. Most companies located there do import bulk goods, convert or assemble into finished, individually packaged units, and ship to offshore customers. As long as sales are not to Panama customers, such companies get a 90 per cent discount from regular corporate income taxes. If your sales are in Panama, you pay full income tax, which is high.

Panama has some limitations, more or less minor depending on the individual considering various tax havens. Persons wanting to set up a trust should look elsewhere, even though technically it is possible to establish one there. Panama, like other Spanish-origin countries, is based on civil law, not English common law. So if you are trust-minded, go to a haven that has a British heritage. Spanish is the official language, but they have a large English-speaking population too. All professional and business executives are bilingual, so language is really no problem. Some observers are concerned about the political situation in Panama, and eventually there could be problems. But it is hard to see how any developments could hurt Panama's tax-haven structure, since it brings the nation such enormous benefits. Furthermore, it is always possible to set up your company for removal on short notice to a safe haven.

Singapore

Singapore is not really a tax haven, even though one could probably set up a non-resident company here that paid no income taxes as long as its business was elsewhere. Our reasons for including Singapore in this list are two: Bank deposits of non-residents there pay no tax on interest: and Asian Currency Units. Similar to Eurodollars, these ACU's are based on a lending fund established by certain western banks to encourage economic expansion. They are also like certificates of deposit in that you buy them in specified amounts and for specific time periods from a minimum of thirty days. For some time now they have been considered one of the best investments in the world, with interest often running higher than 12 per cent, tax free. Singapore residents and Americans cannot buy the ACU's directly; but many are, indirectly, through companies and trusts organized in other countries.

By itself Singapore is of little use as a tax haven. But as an auxiliary or a link in a multinational operation, it can be very important.

Ireland

Some of the highest-tax countries have peculiarities in their tax laws that offer relief under limiting circumstances. Such a country is the Republic of Ireland. Its points of interest in this connection have to do with manufacturing for export, development of Shannon Airport, and the creative output of writers and artists.

If a corporation manufactures goods within the boundaries of the Republic, and if it exports those goods outside the Republic, the income from their sale is not taxed. This feature is of special interest to persons selling to the European Common Market, of which Ireland is a member.

If your enterprise is engaged in certain manufacturing or service activities on the grounds of Shannon International Airport, you pay no tax.

If you write, compose, paint, or sculpt; if you are a resident of Ireland; if your creativity is judged to have artistic or cultural merit; and if you manage to sell it; you pay no tax on your income. Inventors of patents that meet certain requirements enjoy similar benefits.

Costa Rica

This northern neighbor of Panama has tax laws that in many ways are similar to Panama's but probably not superior. In fact, dividends paid by non-resident companies to foreign beneficiaries are taxed at about 5 per cent. Otherwise, such companies pay no taxes. For other details, read the section on Panama. One real advantage in organizing a business in Costa Rica is its very low profile as a tax haven.

What it is best known for in financial circles, probably, is its liberal retirement laws. Foreigners with outside income pay no taxes, have no restrictions placed on them, and reside there indefinitely. As a resident, you can even obtain a Costa Rican passport. To become a resident, you must have a minimum of $300 a month in income (U.S. social security could take care of that requirement), and you must acquire Costa Rican real estate costing at least $10,000. Because of these benefits, and because Costa Rica is the most politically stable country in Latin America and has perhaps the most European-like population, many Americans, Canadians, and Europeans have retired here.

Switzerland

We made earlier reference to Switzerland's discouragement of capital and human influx, except capital in payment for Swiss goods purchased, and humans in the form of free-spending tourists. Foreign investment capital the Swiss do not want if it helps raise the price of their franc. They made this quite clear when they not only stopped paying interest on foreign-owned Swiss francs deposited in their banks, but also imposed a negative interest, or penalty, of about 8 per cent a year. With such measures the Swiss hope to make the price of their goods more competitive in world markets, by reducing the demand for their franc and therefore its relative value. It is all perfectly reasonable and understandable. So is their policy of "Switzerland for the Swiss," which makes it nearly impossible for foreigners to get a work visa or own real estate in Switzerland. (It is also nearly impossible for a Swiss citizen to own real estate there, but because of prices, not laws.)

Switzerland doesn't have to apologize for these measures, not for her tax policies, numbered bank accounts, or anything else. She has an unexcelled record of political and economic stability to wave at detractors, as well as a plausible explanation for the policies mentioned. The Swiss will tell you that their country does not claim to be a tax haven. And when you remove Swiss taxes from a comparison with the so-called tax havens', they suddenly become rather reasonable. Especially in comparison with other industrial nations, Swiss taxes are low. Of course, that is fine for the Swiss but not so fine for the non-Swiss flight capital.

Money is as safe in Swiss banks as anywhere else in the world because of Switzerland's rock-solid stability. Money certainly is not safe from erosion, however, as the Swiss Government compounds the work of inflation by collecting fines from foreign depositors. Otherwise, it is safe from bank failure and from snoopers. Both named and numbered accounts are sanctified by law, deliberate breaches of confidential information being punishable by six months in jail and $20,000. The numbered accounts, by the way, are also necessarily registered by name. The difference is merely in the several top bank officers who alone know the identities of numbered accounts, versus the many bank clerks who can know all the others. The number protects only one's right to privacy; it does not protect against prosecution for illegal activities. Furthermore, numbered bank accounts are not exclusively Swiss. You can get the same service in the Bahamas, Hong Kong, Lebanon, Singapore, Uruguay, Panama or Belgium. A numbered account in Belgium, in fact, would give you virtually the same economic stability as in Switzerland, and fewer raised eyebrows.

Whether one's financial interest in Switzerland is in a bank or a business, there is one vital difference between Swiss attitudes and laws and those of some other countries, most notably the United States. In the U.S., tax evasion—failure to declare all income, for example—is a criminal violation. In Switzerland (and a number of other countries) it is not. For that reason, if the U.S. Internal Revenue Service asks Switzerland for information on an American suspected of not paying all his taxes, the Swiss Government politely refuses, on the grounds that no Swiss law has been broken. A Swiss citizen might be asked by his government to provide documents supporting his tax claims, but the law bars the government from fishing expeditions to dig up hidden information on its taxpayers. It is interesting to note that Switzerland meets all her tax needs without resorting to strongarm methods. The Swiss attitude is that people will voluntarily support reasonable government spending and fair taxation. If the government exceeds the general tolerance level and goodwill of its taxpayers, no number or kind of laws can totally offset the loss of voluntarism. Obviously their policy works, and they simply will not participate with other governments in activities they feel are unnecessary, nonproductive, and with which they basically disagree. They will cooperate in prosecuting tax fraud, however, which is different from tax evasion.

Except for holding companies, which pay low or no taxes, Swiss companies pay taxes up to around 30 per cent. Taxes are on profits and capital. Swiss citizens can apply for refunds, but others pay the full amount, unless the tax is reduced by one of the many treaties Switzerland has with other countries.

There are no trusts, as such, in Switzerland. The two entities most commonly used are the joint stock company and the private limited liability company. Of the two, the joint stock company is the more popular, one reason being that beneficiary shareholders can remain anonymous. All owners of a private limited liability company have to be registered in the Commercial Register; the real owners of a joint stock company do not. There are many details that we could cover about Swiss companies, but one detail makes the others more or less academic, as far as the purpose of this book is concerned. That detail is the amount of subscribed capital required and the amount that has to be paid up in organizing a company. Authorized capital must be at least 50,000 francs (about $20,000), and 20 per cent of that must be paid up, with a minimum of 20,000 francs ($8,000). These figures are not necessarily prohibitive for middle-income investors; but neither are they necessary.

When you compare the tax benefits of some other countries to those of Switzerland, you have to agree that there are better places, especially for the new, inexperienced, and unwealthy investor.

Turks and Caicos Islands

Geographically a part of the Bahamas but politically separate, these are the two most important of seven main islands making up this British Crown Colony. Each has about two thousand of the Colony's seven thousand inhabitants, which is another way of saying that the Colony is small. The biggest employer is the American bases there. There is little industry, little tourism. There are air connections, but not many. There are about 200 companies registered, but no trusts. There could be, since it operates under English common law, but trust laws have not been written yet. The U.S. dollar is the official currency, and there are no exchange controls, no tax treaties, and no taxes. Furthermore, you would probably pay less to start a company here than in any other tax haven and less a year to maintain it. If your authorized capital is less than $2,750, your incorporation fee is only $55 and your annual fee is the same. Your meetings do not have to be held in the Islands, and there are no citizenship or resident requirements for directors, officers, or shareholders.

In short, Turks and Caicos is not fully organized yet, which is either its biggest handicap or its most attractive asset. It does appear to be refreshingly uncomplicated and undemanding and probably is quite suitable for the same kind of business. A fairly sophisticated company might have trouble getting things done. As for privacy, here again you would either go unnoticed because of its relative isolation and provincial status, or you would be more prominent because of the small numbers of companies and people. We cannot make it a top recommendation, but we do think it has intriguing possibilities.

The U.K. and the U.S.

Did you know that foreigners do not pay taxes on interest earned from bank deposits in these countries? A Swiss, for example, pays no tax on interest earned by his savings account in a New York or a London bank. Among the foreigners earning tax-free interest in U.K. banks, however, do not include U.S. citizens. They are supposed to pay taxes on interest earned anywhere; and that makes Americans among the most heavily and restrictively taxed citizens in the world—unless they take steps to avoid some of their taxes. Perhaps you are beginning to get some inkling of ways this can be accomplished. It will be much clearer to you as you continue to read.

4 Proprietorship, Partnership, Corporation, Trust

In talking about the various tax havens, we have necessarily touched on the business and financial entities that constitute free enterprise wherever it operates. Eventually, if not regularly, we are all a direct or indirect participant in all these entitles— proprietorships, partnerships, corporations, trusts—and in most if not all the variations of each. Most persons have never been involved in the creation of any kind of business entity (if we exclude baby-sitting, lemonade stands and lawn-mowing services), and few persons have ever helped organize every kind of business entity that exists.

For most of us, therefore, a quick review is in order at this point. After all, if you are somewhat hazy or outright ignorant about the fundamentals of a corporation or a trust, how can you determine what arrangement will work best for you in reducing your tax load? We do not suggest that you will be an expert in corporate law at the conclusion of this chapter. You will know enough after reading this book, however, to set an intelligent course for yourself. And you can then benefit from the work of experts who have already set up the machinery and who will handle the details of your enterprise, subject to your approval.

An excellent book on the U.S. Corporation which includes comparisons between other legal entitles and with usable tear-out forms is "How to Form Your Own Corporation Without A Lawyer for Under $50" by Ted Nicholas. It is published by Enterprise Publishing, Inc., and the sales price is $14.95.

Actually, a pure definition for each entity probably cannot be written. The differences between a proprietorship, a partnership, and a corporation, for example, are not found in a comparison of size or method of daily operation. A corporation can be essentially a one-man operation, and a proprietorship can employ hundreds. From a practical standpoint, a small proprietorship and a small corporation have more in common than a small and a large corporation. Furthermore, the line of demarcation between one kind of corporation and another, or between one kind of trust and another, is sometimes vague. Disputes even arise on the difference, in a given case, between a corporation and a trust. Many persons including the author could modify, qualify, and expand the following review, but beyond a point, the attempts at clarification only confuse the reader who is not sophisticated about such matters. Additional detail is available from many sources, should you feel the need for it. If you become really serious about organizing a foreign-based company, you will undoubtedly check a number of other sources for supplemental and confirming information, although such checking is not prerequisite to organizing your foreign-based business. Ultimately, you will exchange references with your agents in the tax haven or havens of your choice. *Everyone needs confidence in his business associates*, and your agents will require evidence of your integrity as you will of theirs.

The Methods of Organizing a Business:

Proprietorship. This is the simplest form of business entity. You need no documents to set it up and none to discontinue it. You hold no meetings and have no arguments about how to run the business—at least no internal arguments of legal import, except perhaps with your spouse. It is less formal, less complicated, and often pays lower taxes than corporations. If you hire help, however, you escape little of the red tape required of a corporation of like size. *Furthermore, you are personally liable for all debts and obligations of your business*, and this is probably your most serious handicap as a sole proprietor. Another potential problem is what happens to the business if the proprietor dies or is incapacitated.

Note: A proprietorship really has no place in a tax-saving plan involving foreign tax havens. The principal argument against it for U.S. citizens is its inability to qualify legally as an alien enterprise, thereby escaping the full burden of domestic taxation.

Partnership. This form of business involves some advantages and some disadvantages not present in a proprietorship or a corporation. Usually, a partner or several partners add financial strength to the business. They might also add talent and experience. They might even provide the extra labor that will preclude the hiring of extra help and the resulting involvement with government bureaus. Nevertheless, they still suffer the same handicaps as the proprietorship regarding legal obligations and at least one additional negative feature. *The partners are personally liable for all the debts and other responsibilities of the business. Furthermore, each partner is responsible for the actions of the other partners in conducting the business.* If your partner makes a bad decision, even without your knowledge, you are fully responsible for the consequences. If he absconds with all your assets, you will still be required to settle accounts with suppliers, tax collectors, and customers, or get relief through bankruptcy if you are unable to meet the obligations.

As for tax benefits in a partnership established in some foreign tax haven, you should forget it, especially if you are a U.S. citizen. For U.S. tax purposes your business will still be a domestic business, subject to the same taxes as it would be if situated in your home town. Because proprietors and partners are individually responsible for their respective enterprises, and because U.S. citizens are almost without exception taxed on their income from any location on earth, the only recourse with these forms of business is to change one's citizenship. For most Americans that is not only unthinkable, it is also nearly impossible.

Corporation. This is a fast-growing form of business entity for a number of very good reasons. The rules governing the ownership, management, and beneficiaries of a corporation vary from country to country and from state to state within a country. And different countries identify them in different ways. But there is a common denominator that groups them all together and represents their most important feature: *limited liability. Your liability is limited to the amount of your investment in the company.*

There are other benefits, however. A corporation shares some of the advantages of a partnership in the additional capital and greater variety of talent represented by more than one owner. If, through death or incapacity, you are unable to continue actively in operating the company, the business can survive without you. So your family can continue to benefit from your investment either as a shareholder receiving dividends or through the sale of your shares in the company. The ownership through shares can be a boom also to the owner who wants to get out of the business for whatever reason. He doesn't have to liquidate the whole company to do so.

There can be some tax advantages, too, in such matters as accumulating earnings in the business to defer taxes until a more favorable period. There also are ways to save money by transferring certain expenses to the corporation as a cost of doing business and by partially financing the corporation through loans you make to it. In the latter instance, repayment of the loan interest is a business expense for the corporation, and so reduces the corporation's taxable earnings, and thereby its taxes, and you pay no taxes on the repaid principal because it is not income but repayment of a loan. If you instead received additional shares for your investment, the earnings of the corporation would be taxed twice—once, on corporate profits (or perhaps higher property taxes if it is reinvested) and again on the dividends you (as a shareholder) receive from those earnings. To make a loan legitimate, however, the corporation has to pay you interest, which is a tax deduction for the corporation but taxable income for you (as an individual). But that still works out to a net benefit for you as sole owner or co-owner of the business. But be careful of getting carried away. The Government will look askance at your lending money to your corporation in a ratio of loans-to-investment greater than three to one. *A foreign-based corporation, on the other hand, will enable you to use this device much more liberally than that.* There are other benefits from a corporation besides the ones mentioned, and there are some disadvantages as well.

We mentioned the disadvantage of double-taxation. Another might be what was mentioned as an asset: limited liability. That feature can cause suppliers to refuse opening a line of credit to a new corporation—a problem that can sometimes be overcome by giving them a personal guarantee.

But oftentimes a supplier, who is after all in competition with other suppliers, will simply take the risk. The easy transfer of ownership can also be a problem. If your shares sell on the open market, you can find yourself in association with persons whose ideas are at conflict with your own. Even if you or your close associates control a majority of the stock, incompatible factions can cause you trouble. And of course if you do not retain majority ownership, you could lose control of the company. Even if you do not sell shares in the stock market, one of your corporate partners might sell his shares to someone you would not choose for a business partner. You can avoid this problem, though, by insisting at the outset on a "buy-and-sell" agreement (sometimes known as a "right of first refusal") that prohibits the sale of shares to outsiders unless the other shareholders are first given a chance to buy them. This would apply, of course, only in a closed corporation (which usually, by law, can have only about 15 shareholders at most), which is one whose stock is not traded on the open market.

The Goal: Privacy

One other possible disadvantage in a corporation is really one of the main advantages of a foreign-based corporation. And that is privacy. In most countries and most states of the United States, the laws require corporations to file an annual report, and often the report must be posted in public places. Naturally, every shareholder of a publicly-traded stock receives a financial report that includes the name and compensation for each officer. So even without your broadcasting the information any further, many strangers have access to details that you might prefer to keep confidential. Even closed corporations have to file reports containing the same information; and even though these reports are not broadly distributed, neither do the various governments involved make any special effort to protect their contents from the curious.

There is in fact, very little information of any kind in the United States these days that can be protected from prying eyes. Even sensitive information affecting national security is demanded under the dual cries of "right to know" and "freedom of the press." So what chance does a poor businessman have to keep his private affairs from anyone who persists in seeing them? Foreigners are amazed at the kind of information that freely changes hands in the U.S., largely as a result of the plastic money explosion. Everything except perhaps the details of one's sex life is passed among creditors like so many schoolboy trading cards.

It would also amaze many Americans to learn, conversely, how tightly-guarded private financial information is in other countries. The names and entries of bank accounts are not the only information that is protected by law and tradition, either. As you have already noted on preceding pages, in many countries the names of real shareholders and directors need not be disclosed in annual reports; and in several countries, annual reports are not even required. It is even possible in at least one country to change the capitalization and the directors of a corporation without reporting the changes. In countries that permit bearer shares, moreover, ownership of a corporation can change hands literally in just seconds, with no one outside the parties involved knowing anything about it. The person having possession of a share or shares of a company is the legal owner (provided he didn't steal them) of the shares and of that much of the company. All of this is to say that a lack of privacy is a corporation drawback only in some countries, not in the best tax havens.

We make so much of that point because corporations, along with trusts, are the key to the use of a tax haven. The essential point is that a corporation is a legal person. If the corporation is established as a foreign corporation, it is in effect a foreign citizen, regardless of the nationality of its founders, officers or directors. It is beyond the legal reach of other countries, and only its business activities within another country can in any way be regulated by that country.

This is how a U.S. citizen, for example, for tax purposes can become a foreign citizen without relinquishing his U.S. citizenship. He handles it through his foreign corporation (or trust) or through several corporations (and/or trusts) in a tiered or multinational arrangement. As long as his gains are not attributable to him, they are not taxable by the U.S. or his state government. And if the corporation and its source(s) of income are located in no-tax or low-tax countries, the gains and profits pay no taxes or low taxes. *It is even possible in some cases for the foreign corporation to earn money from activities in the U.S. without paying any U.S. taxes on them*, or at least not until the earnings are taken out of the corporation and repatriated, or brought into the U.S., for the American shareholder's personal benefit. Even at this point many persons bring in money tax free. Some of them do it by strictly legal means; some by technically legal means; and others by means that circumvent the rules as presently written, while qualifying on a personal code of justice and morality vis-a-vis waste, corruption, and unfairness in the handling of tax revenues.

We are not here to tell you exactly how to invest your money or how to take your earnings. To reiterate, we are writing this book to inform you on the ways tax havens can be used and are being used to reduce a large amount of the tax burden now being carried by the productive segment of the industrial nations. And, of course, we are not urging the violation of the laws of any state or nation. We'll get into the details as soon as we cover a few more points on corporations and deal with the subject of trusts.

So far, we have talked about the pros and cons of a corporation, but we have not said anything about the procedures for organizing one. The subject strikes many persons as a heavy and expensive mystery, and it is important to understand that incorporating a company requires neither large sums of money nor superior intelligence nor a high-powered and expensive lawyer. Actually, you could skip over all this and, once you've decided to incorporate a Cayman or Hong Kong corporation, merely fill out the confidential information form contained later in this book, enclose a check for the required fees, and in short while you would receive your charter or certificate of incorporation. We offer the information here partly to show you how relatively uncomplicated the steps in incorporation can be and to make the point that incorporating in a foreign country is virtually the same as at home.

A Short Digression

Before going any further discussing corporations, we should touch on the term, "company." To most persons this word connotes corporation. But because it can mean a proprietorship or a partnership as well as a corporation, it is not usually accepted as a legal designation of incorporation. You can refer to it as the XYZ Company, but if it is a corporation, letterheads and official company forms should say "XYZ Corporation" or "XYZ, Inc." In British or formerly British countries, you will have to use the term "Limited" or its abbreviation. French and Spanish countries use the initials "S.A.," meaning "anonymous society." In Germany you would use "AG."

Speaking of companies, you have seen us use the terms "investment company" and "holding company." Whether it is a corporation or other kind of company, both of them deal primarily or totally in investments. The difference is in the word "control." An *investment company*, such as a mutual fund, carries a portfolio of shares in a number of different companies and holds no controlling share in any of them. Or it might invest in something besides corporation stock. A *holding company*, on the other hand, holds at least a majority share of another company's stock or several companies' stock. A holding company is also referred to as a parent company, and the companies it owns or controls as subsidiary or wholly-owned companies.

How To Do It

Following are the basic requirements in the formation of the U.S. corporation. These requirements apply whether it is a large company listed on the New York Stock Exchange or one in which all the officers and directors are family members or close friends, and the stock is all held by the same persons or by one owner. The difference would be in the detail involved for each.

1. Decide which state you will incorporate in. Some states have more liberal incorporation laws than others. Since you don't have to incorporate in your own state, you might find Delaware, the state most friendly to corporations and with the most advantages, a better choice. This is also the first step in creating a foreign corporation, although your criteria will differ somewhat.

2. Choose a name for your company. It can be any name that doesn't conflict with local laws or with another company competing in the

same markets. In most instances it will have to identify itself as a corporation. You will probably submit second and third choices in case your first or second is unacceptable. The same requirements apply to a foreign-based corporation.

3. Decide on the kind of stock to issue and how to distribute it. All corporations issue common stock, and some also issue preferred stock. Unless you have some reason for issuing fixed-dividend, non-voting stock, your small corporation will do as most small corporations do and stick to common stock. Even so, you still have a choice to make. Depending on your particular jurisdiction, you can issue shares with a par value or no-par value, that are voting or non-voting and even a special kind called Section 1244 Stock. The voting feature is self-explanatory. Par value, theoretically, is the total capitalization divided by the number of shares issued. These numbers can be whatever the incorporators want them to be (subject to any laws governing allowable minimums). Since par value does not usually reflect the market value of a share, the trend is toward shares marked "no par value." Section 1244 Stock permits shareholders in small corporations to deduct from personal income the full amount of investment losses up to $50,000 a year ($100,000 on joint returns). Without this qualification you get to deduct only part of your capital losses.

As for distribution of the shares, they can be divided among the incorporators, officers, directors, and anyone else in any mutually agreeable apportionment. Or they might be held by one person only. In fact it is a good idea not to issue all the stock but to hold some of it as "treasury stock" so you can take on additional stockholders or award bonuses without having to alter your charter. Furthermore, since the filing fee is often determined by the number of shares issued, it is wise to keep the number small.

Foreign corporations (based outside the U.S.), generally require the same decisions regarding their stock. We have mentioned one exception that allows greater flexibility and privacy in a corporation's affairs, and that is the bearer share allowed by some countries. Some or all of the stock in an exempt Cayman Islands corporation, for example, can be issued as bearer shares, but the details must be included in the articles of incorporation.

4. Your charter or certificate of incorporation will usually include the following:

    a. The name of the corporation.
    b. The address of its principal office.
    c. The purpose of the corporation. This should be stated broadly so as not to restrict its operations and growth.
    d. The class or classes of stock to be issued, how it may be paid for, the number of shares in each class, and their par value.
    e. The amount of authorized capital and the amount of indebtedness the corporation is authorized to incur.
    f. The number of directors.
    g. The names and addresses of directors and officers.
    h. The names of shareholders, their addresses, the classes and numbers of shares held.

    The charter or certificate of incorporation is likewise basic to all foreign corporations and generally must contain the same information.

5. Most states (U.S. and foreign) do not require a corporation to have by-laws, but most companies have them anyhow. The by-laws state the operating rules of the company in detail as specific as the incorporators and directors wish. They might be prepared at the same time as the charter or as one of the first orders of business after the charter is issued. Typical by-laws would include in addition to the information in the charter:

    a. Disposition of stock, first-refusal rights of purchase, status of treasury stock.
    b. Time and location of stockholder meetings, including annual and special meetings, notice requirements, power to remove directors or change by-laws, proxy (absentee) voting rights and procedures, who shall preside at meetings, and other matters pertaining to meetings.
    c. The functions and powers of directors, organization of the

board, requirements of director meetings, definition of a quorum for making decisions, etc.

d. What officers the corporation will have, how they will be removed and replaced, their duties and powers.

e. How and when dividends are to be decided and declared, where the corporate funds are to be kept and requirements for withdrawals and disbursements.

Such formality in a small corporation will seem silly to some persons, and indeed by-laws for a very small compatible group of persons can be superfluous. As all of us know, however, strong differences of opinion can occur even within a family. And the existence of by-laws can at such times remove much of the emotion in a dispute by providing a government of law and not of men.

6. The charter is submitted, along with the required fees, to the secretary of state or other designated authority. That office might request additional information, but otherwise it will in due time (usually several weeks) issue notice of acceptance. A copy of the charter is often filed with the county clerk, and the corporation is officially in business.

7. It is wise, and often required, to keep a minutes book. In it the company secretary records all important details of stockholder and director meetings, including capital investments or divestitures, loans made and received, acquisitions, mergers, purchases and sales of capital equipment and real estate, changes in by-laws, annual reports, and so forth.

8. It is also important to keep orderly records. All financial transactions should be kept and balanced regularly. Even though this is sound practice for every person and every business, it is particularly important for a corporation to maintain neat files and ledgers. Otherwise, all persons not involved in the transactions, but having a right to know, cannot be informed. Moreover, a corporation is involved in matters peculiar to its organization and methods of operation.

As for the actual documents used informing and operating a corporation, there is no set form or specific wording required as long as the information you want and the state requires is included. To get the words on paper, you can follow either of two courses, or both. You can hire a lawyer to write the documents for you; you can use model forms verbatim or with whatever alterations you care to make; or you can follow the model forms and then have a lawyer go over them. There is nothing wrong with using model forms. Lawyers themselves fall into set forms and in effect follow their own and other lawyers' models. You can buy a "corporation kit" from many stationery stores or their suppliers. They usually cost about $35 and contain sample charters and by-laws to fill in or follow, a corporation seal for your company alone, stock certificates ready for names and numbers, a minutes book, a stock book to record shareholders, and often model notes, resolutions, minutes, and agreements.

You can get the same kind of help from business agents in the different foreign tax havens. For your convenience, the names and addresses of experienced and reliable agents for the Cayman Islands and for Hong Kong are contained later in this book. We have also given you a simple confidential information form that you can fill out and send to your agent, bank, or trust company in your chosen haven. Our whole point in describing the requirements of a corporation is to bring you close enough to the subject to see it as a practical reality for you and, further, to make the process of incorporating a foreign-based company an easier matter for you than it would be otherwise.

Trust. The term "trust" can sound even more formidable than the term "corporation." It needn't, however, for a trust is not necessarily more complicated than a corporation—or necessarily any simpler. For the non-legal person what makes all kinds of documents mind-numbing is the archaic language in which they are written along with the attempt to plug all verbal leaks so that slippery scoundrels can't sneak through. Unfortunately, by the time the ancient phrases have been strung together with daisy chains of cover-everything verbs, nouns, pronouns, adjectives, prepossitions, and conjunctions, most of us are lost at the third turn. Tradition dies hard, and often that is very good. Some traditions should never die. But some wag has said about the legalese tradition that it is kept alive by a profession that wouldn't be kept alive without it.

Anyhow, a trust is essentially just an arrangement by which one person or group of persons entrusts money or property to another person or group for the benefit of a third person or group. You hear the words *creator, grantor, donor, settlor,* or *trustor*—all words meaning the same thing: the person or institution that creates or initiates the trust. Then you encounter a couple of Latin words: *res* for "thing" and *corpus,* meaning "body." Even in English they don't tell you anything until some translator explains that they stand for the assets (money or property) granted by the grantor (donated by the donor) to benefit the third person or party. If the trust property is money or something easily negotiable, the trust "res" is sometimes called the *trust fund.* The trust fund is entrusted to the *trustee.* This is the person or institution selected by the grantor to safeguard and administer the trust fund.

In a way, the trustee is like a godfather or godmother. There are many ways in which a trust can work, but the usual purpose of one is to provide for a wife, children, or grandchildren after the breadwinner has died or become incapacitated. It is to ensure that a competent administrator will handle the trust fund according to the wishes of the grantor to benefit persons he cares about. Not only does a trust take care of minors, widows, and irresponsible heirs, it can also help the wholly capable adult beneficiary.

One of its main contributions is a whopping tax savings to both the grantor and the beneficiaries. U.S. law allows limited tax exemptions on gifts or contributions; so the grantor can give up to $3,000 a year for each beneficiary. The $30,000 lifetime gift tax exemption and the $60,000 estate tax exemption have been replaced by a single unified credit. Thus, the part of the credit which can be used by the estate of a decedent is reduced to the extent that the unified credit was used by the decedent during his life to offset *gift* taxes. The amount of this unified credit is as follows:

For 1980, the amount of credit is $42,500.

For 1981, and years thereafter, the amount of the credit is $47,000.

There are legal time limits on all but charity trusts, the benefits and tax savings can extend to third generation and further, if the planner is clever.

But using a trust in conjunction with a will is just one way to benefit from a trust. The trust that takes effect on the grantor's death is called a "testamentary trust." There is also a "living trust," often called *inter vivos* by lawyers. This is one that functions during the grantor's lifetime and can continue afterward. Among other uses, the living trust is growing in popularity with estate planners who want to avoid the long delays and higher costs of putting a will through probate court. Since the trust is already in effect at the grantor's death, no transfer of assets is required after death, and therefore no probate is necessary or required.

Some of the tax breaks given to trusts are based upon the technical surrender of assets by the grantor. In setting up a trust, one passes title to and relinquishes control of those assets. The title and management is legally given to the trustee who, cannot however, be taxed on any part of it except his income from administration fees because he never receives any of the principal or its earnings. By the same token, the beneficiary cannot be taxed until the trust fund is distributed to him. Even then, if the beneficiary is a minor or is retired, he will pay little or no tax on the distribution of assets. This shifting of income from a high tax bracket to a low bracket through a living trust is quite a common practice. By this measure, for example, fathers help sons get started in business, the sons paying lower taxes on income from trust property than their fathers would on the same income from the same property.

Some persons, despite the benefits provided by trusts, do not like the idea of signing away the title and management of large equities for the rest of their lives or even for a stipulated period. Even though the trustee is reliable and bound by law to act prudently and conscientiously, he is not required to take orders from the grantor. Also, the grantor might change his mind about what he wants the trust to do, or conditions might change. Trusts created for business purposes especially cannot always be bound to a fixed policy and course. For whatever reasons, within the classification of living trusts are the sub-classifications "irrevocable trust" and "revocable trust." An irrevocable trust is looked upon much more kindly by tax collectors and certainly is the safer way to go. And a time limit can be set for any trust when the instrument, or paper, is first drawn up.

Because of their great flexibility and because they enjoy some tax privileges not granted to corporations, trusts have become very useful in business. Trusts originated centuries ago in the common law of England, and even today they are a practical instrument only in those countries, including the U.S., whose laws are based on English common law. Business trusts are primarily an American development. They originated in Massachusetts around the middle of the last century as a result of that state's refusal to let corporations deal in real estate. They spread rapidly to other states during the early years of this century when many of the states imposed harsh burdens and restrictions on corporate activities, particularly on out-of-state corporations.

In many respects a trust is like a corporation. It can buy and sell, make investments, own property, hold assets, organize business entities, liquidate them, perform services, and distribute earnings, among other things. It can also accumulate earnings for distribution later, and when one is set up specifically for this purpose, it is called an *accumulation trust*. Among foreign-based business entities, a trust can do this job with surer tax benefits than a corporation, which likewise can accumulate earings. Like a corporation also, a business trust enjoys limited liability: Only the trust property is vulnerable to creditors, not the shareholders or the trustees. However, under some circumstances a foreign entity which accumulates income may cause shareholders or beneficiaries to pay taxes on such income whether distributed or not.

The main distinction between a business trust and a corporation is that matter of control. Whereas the beneficiaries of a corporation can and do control the enterprise, the beneficiaries of a trust are not allowed to. If, by the trust deed or the actions of the shareholders and beneficiaries, the trustees are managed, appointed, or removed, the courts will treat the organization as a partnership and tax it accordingly. Technically, that appears to be a large and serious mark against the use of trusts in business. From a practical standpoint, however, it usually is not. After all, the trustee is chosen for compatibility with the aims of the trust's creator. Furthermore, a trustee would normally have no reason for managing the trust in a way contrary to the wishes of the creators and beneficiaries. (The creators, or grantors, and the beneficiaries might be different or they might be the same. The trust is on firmer tax-benefit ground if they are not the same.) Theoretically the trustee owns the property and administers it independently; but because he (or they) cannot profit from the property, there is no temptation to steer a different course. Usually, in fact, the trustee will welcome suggestions from the grantors and beneficiaries. And anything short of a direct command is quite legitimate. So the real principals of a trust will periodically send a "memorandum of wishes" to the trustee to guide his hand in their interest. Unless their wishes are clearly illegal, the institution acting as trustee will strive to protect its reputation as a cooperative and able trust manager. After all, it is in competition with other trust-managing firms and cannot afford to have people say that it is difficult to deal with.

Now that we have reviewed the principal foreign tax havens and the business entities one might consider using for the tax advantages of a haven, we can move next to specific ways in which tax havens can be used to reduce or even eliminate taxes. At this point we must make clear that we will not be telling you specifically what business you should enter. Because the possibilities are almost infinite and because no one knows better than you what you can do and what to do, any suggestions from us would be arbitrary, capricious, and presumptuous. If you really want suggestions or information on business opportunities, you can always get help from the local banks, commercial and tourism development offices, or even newspapers from the havens that interest you. A starting place could be the embassy of each country in your national capital. We will talk about manufacturing, sales, investments, services, dividends, royalties, interest, and so on. If we mention actual products, services, or investments, it will be for examples only and not direct suggestions. If you already have a business of your own, of course, you will be reading to learn how you might transfer it to a foreign base and perhaps double your profits. No promises, but we sure say that there are enough possibilities to justify your time to read and think about.

5 The Different Ways Tax Havens Are Used

First of all, let us acknowledge that there are ways to reduce taxes *in your own country*. In some years, many persons—even in the United States—manage to pay no taxes at all, and quite legally. There are ways that the informed and alert can reduce their tax burdens; and they are not only allowed to do so, it is a personal duty to themselves to do so. No less than the U.S. Supreme Court has said as much. Justice Learned Hand is often quoted on the subject: "Anyone may so arrange his affairs that taxes shall be as low as possible; he is not bound to choose that pattern which will best pay the treasury; it is not even a patriotic duty to increase one's taxes." The Court has also said: ". . . the legal right of a taxpayer to decrease the amount of what otherwise would be his taxes, or to altogether avoid them by means which the law permits, cannot be doubted."

Unfortunately, the opportunities to avoid taxes in most of the world's industrialized nations are inexorably shrinking. The tax rates themselves are reduced from time to time as the government tinkers with the nation's economy, but the long-range direction has been upward and undoubtedly will continue in this direction indefinitely. Even in years when the rates are reduced, the so-called loopholes written into the tax code to achieve certain desirable effects are also reduced in number or degree. The persons who cause these reductions claim to be benefiting the little man at the expense of the wealthy, although it should be obvious that the destruction of incentives for the ambitious, industrious, and talented can only hurt the persons who depend on the industry produced by that drive and talent. Nevertheless, it is not obvious to enough voters, so at last the productive segment is casting eyes elsewhere—to tax havens—for incentives to keep producing.

And what do they find? They find *other* governments quite willing to let them keep virtually all their profits as long as their business activities also produce gains for those governments and their citizens that they would not otherwise receive. Unfortunately, their enlightened attitudes and policies are not enough by themselves to help the refugee taxpayer, especially the American refugee. The man from the "protection agency" (the IRS) still makes his rounds every quarter demanding his percentage. So what does the refugee do? He changes his citizenship—not actually, but by proxy. He forms a foreign corporation or trust in a country that is friendly toward business. You might say he becomes twins, one twin retaining his native citizenship, the other twin becoming a citizen (actually, a non-human *entity*) of the friendly tax country. The latter twin, of course, is the foreign-based corporation or trust that is recognized by the laws of both countries as a legal "person." It can do almost anything and have almost anything done to it legally that a real person can do or have done to him legally. That is the first step. What steps he takes next, when and how he takes them, and what kinds of business he engages in will determine whether, when, and how much tax he and his twin back home will pay.

You see, it is not enough to be a citizen of a foreign country, located in a foreign country, and doing business in a foreign country. If the alien company earns a certain minimum of certain kinds of income, and if it is owned by a certain number of U.S. citizens, the long arm of the Internal Revenue Service will reach out and take its cut of the owners' shares whether they receive the income or leave it with the company.

Be not dismayed, however, for we did not come this far only to shrug and say "Uncle". Many U.S. taxpayers have looked at such a situation and said: All right, if the IRS wants to take dominion over everything that moves on the face of the earth, we will obey the letter of the Codes but observe the spirit of our own codes. And so U.S. citizens, *through their foreign companies*, have collected interest and rents, have performed services, manufactured and sold goods, collected royalties, have bought and sold property, transported goods, and collected dividends, and *have managed to pay no taxes or sharply reduced taxes on the profits.*

How, you ask, other than by screening their connections and failing to declare their beneficiary status and income? Undoubtedly many persons have held on to their gains in just that way. After all, the IRS can audit only a small percentage of the hundred-million conventional returns each year. There is a lot of random checking, but most of the audits occur only when some item on a return disturbs the normal patterns. IRS investigators have their hands full just spot-checking and running down pattern exceptions. There is hardly any extra time or manpower to go rummaging through public records in the hope that something might turn up, especially if the records are in foreign lands. (Of course, if the IRS is out to get someone, no holds are barred.)

That is why some experts advise foreign-based companies to refrain from conducting any business whatever *in the U.S.* Such a company is allowed to buy unimproved real estate in the U.S. and sell it at a gain without paying any tax. But this action gives the IRS a hook to hang an investigation on. Once they can establish a connection between a U.S. citizen and a foreign company, they hold all the aces if he has been derelict in his tax returns. There is an important "hook"—and an important trap.

Let's suppose, however, that barber Tony Barbiere in Queens, New York, has organized a corporation in the Cayman Islands to manufacture and sell men's hair spray. He calls his company Amore (since it is an exempt company he does not have to use the term "Limited"). His exempt status, which gives him maximum privacy along with guaranteed long-term freedom from any future Cayman taxes, nevertheless does not permit his company to operate in the Cayman Islands; but the location is not ideal for aerosol manufacturing and sales anyhow. So he establishes an Amore branch in Nassau, Bahamas; he invests $5,000 in equipment, materials, and start-up overhead, and begins making hair spray in a rented cinder-block garage.

He is still in Queens, remember, cutting hair and placing bets. He has set up his company in both locations without having gone to either place. The directors, shareholders, and officers of Amore are named, let's say, Charles Hammer, John Donaldson, and Peter

Worth. They are nominee directors provided by his agent in George Town, C.I. Tony has a bank account in George Town listed under the company name, and his checks can be countersigned by his agent. Tony also has a manager in Nassau to supervise the two workers in his "plant" and to handle the routine details.

Tony can sell his hair spray in Nassau and Freeport and pay no taxes on his profits because the Bahamas have no income taxes. But that is not a very big market for men's hair spray. So he sets up another corporation, this one in the Bahamas, to sell his hair spray. He calls it "Groom, Ltd.," and once again he uses nominee directors, officers, and shareholders. Note that Amore, being a "person," can be one of the incorporators and beneficiary shareholders. Amore makes hair spray for 75 cents a can and sells it to Groom, Ltd., for $1.50. Groom ships to sales agents throughout Latin America for $1.50 plus freight and import duties. He gives the agents 25 cents a can of the $1.50, thereby grossing 50 cents and netting a profit of 25 cents. Even if he has sales branches in countries that tax profits, like the U.S., he pays no corporate income tax because Groom, Ltd., has made no profit. And he pays no tax on the 25-cents profit Amore made from its sales to Groom, Ltd., because there are no taxes in the Bahamas. Furthermore, Groom can sell Amore hair spray in the Cayman Islands, which Amore could not as an exempt company (could as an ordinary company).

So far, so good. He sells 100,000 cans of Amore hair spray the third year for a net profit of $25,000. His initial investment of perhaps $10,000 has been paid off, and from now on it is all gravy—IF the IRS will leave him alone. If Amore were a U.S. corporation, it might pay about $4,500 in corporate taxes on its year's profits. If Tony took his profits as salary or dividends, he would pay a personal income tax. And, if Tony's corporation is deemed to be a "Controlled Foreign Corporation," he—as a stockholder—would pay taxes on the income, *whether or not the income was distributed!*

The Chance of IRS Hassles

First, let's talk about the odds for and against a tete-a-tete with the Internal Revenue. Whether or not Tony has told the IRS about his foreign business, the real moment of truth might not come until he tries to lay his hands on his accumulating money. Long before he takes the first step to establish a foreign company he will have to ponder some options available to him. There are ways and there are ways, but we will deal with the most obvious first.

He can, of course, leave his money in the Cayman Islands and take himself (and his family) there to spend it; or he can do some traveling with the money, even back to the U.S. The law allows him to bring in or take out as much as $5,000 at a time without declaring it. He better watch out, though, if he has anything to hide, because there is nothing like a jealous neighbor for getting a man into trouble with the tax collectors. (And, if this money is "attributed" to him, he would be liable for taxes on it.) If the IRS knows about Tony's corporation, it can demand records, and then Tony will have to pay U.S. taxes plus fines on the money he spent traveling or risk charges of tax evasion or fraud if he doesn't declare that money.

Let's say that Tony, while cutting hair in his Queens barbershop, makes the mistake of talking about his Cayman Island vacations. One of his patrons—just for spite, or for money paid by the IRS for such stool pigeons—tells the IRS that there is something funny going on because four-dollar haircuts don't pay a family's way to the Caribbean several times a year. The IRS gets crank calls like these in multitudes, and, when they require extensive foreign travel, can only afford to investigate tips involving *substantial* tax evasion. After all, even the Government has to look at the potential return on its investment every now and then!

Let's say that an IRS man flies to Grand Cayman to sniff around. He goes to the Registrar of Companies and looks through the corporations and the names of their directors, officers, and shareholders. No "Tony Barbiere" is mentioned anywhere. He suspects that Barbiere might have a corporation named "Amore" because he noticed a can of hair spray labeled Amore in Barbiere's shop, and the manufacturer was in Grand Cayman. "Aha!"—or so the IRS snooper thinks. He finds a corporation named Amore registered, but the only names listed for it are those of three men named Hammer, Donaldson, and Worth. The IRS man questions all three, but they never heard of a Tony Barbiere.

The IRS snooper makes the rounds of the banks, identifying himself and asking for information. The bank officers politely reply that they are not allowed to discuss such private matters. They cannot even tell him whether Mr. Barbier has an account there, much less how much is in it. They also will not discuss any banking performed by the Amore Company.

The IRS man makes one last try. He goes to the Law Courts, saying he is investigating a report that an American has income from a Cayman corporation that he has not declared. But tax evasion in the Cayman Islands and many other countries is *not* a violation of law. They tell him that they cannot cooperate because no *Cayman* law has been broken.

As a result of all these rejections, the IRS man has *no evidence* on which to base a charge and can only hope that Barbiere will admit his omission when asked the question directly. With nothing more than that to go on, however, it is a toss-up whether he would pursue the matter any further.

Why doesn't anyone in the Caymans cooperate? The bank officer and the Court official are not normally uncooperative types. Even though no local laws have been broken, they would ordinarily provide information in response to a polite request, especially from a U.S. Government representative on official business. In this case, however, the banker is strongly motivated to refuse information. *If he discloses confidential information and is found out, he will be subject to fine and imprisonment, not to mention destruction of his reputation and career.* Only if there is a clear indication of fraud may the laws on privacy be by-passed, but the banker has nothing to gain by talking and possibly everything to lose. Behind the law and even beyond the moral issue of privacy rights lies the over-riding interest of the community. The very welfare of the Islands depends on maintaining a friendly, protective environment for investment capital. When the wolf enters the meadow, the herd draws together warily for mutual protection. When a tax hunter comes to any tax haven, the word goes out fast, and quickly the circle is closed to him. He is intruding his harsh and alien policy into a sovereignty that does not agree with it. And, as a matter of fact, because of this uniform opposition to fishing expeditions from high-tax nations, the fishermen usually stay home. Without tangible evidence from the Cayman government and banks involved, there is little left short of confession by the suspect on which the IRS could hang a case.

If there is any "secret" to a successful tax haven entity—be it corporation, partnership, or trust—this "secret" is the lack of knowledge on the part of the nominal directors, partners, or trustees of the persons behind the entity. The law regarding tax havens is strict, as is pointed out in Chapter 1. But mere allegations as to what the IRS believed is "really going on" *must be proved*. Let's suppose, however, that Tony is a worrier, and even though he disagrees with the tax codes, he doesn't want to be forever looking over his shoulder. So, as required by law, within ninety days after receiving his certificate of incorporation from the Cayman Registrar of Companies, he files Form 959 with the IRS. He has decided that everything he does will be legally defensible. But he knows there will be areas of interpretation, and he wants to avert frequent haggling with the tax office. The tax people are paid to haggle; he is not.

To steer clear of time-wasting debates, therefore, he decides to travel by water rather than by land. The trip will be the same, but he won't be bothered by chatty tax men who see his tracks and catch up to make conversation. He will use nominee directors instead of posting his name; he will conduct his affairs through his foreign manager and agents; he will issue bearer shares so that ownership can be transferred quickly and easily and without requiring records. In these and other ways he will use legal technicalities to avoid roadblocks just as the lawyers and judges do in criminal charge dismissals.

Being Cautious

If a tax investigator will arbitrarily refuse to allow a small casualty claim that is clearly allowable under the tax laws, what position will he take in a gray area like "arm's-length" transactions? Technically, Tony's arrangement to avoid taxes on profits from his hair spray business was legal. A tax man could call it subterfuge, however, asserting that the deal between the two companies was not transacted at "arm's-length." His argument would be more persuasive if the relationship were between companies of the same name in different countries or different names in the same country. What constitutes arm's length? What constitutes a valid casualty claim? Often it is a matter of which investigator reviews the claim and what he had for breakfast. Since the best that a taxpayer can expect from an audit is the same as he would have realized without the audit, and the worst is something he shouldn't think about, the Low Profile is next to the best protection. Invisibility is the best "profile."

Near-invisibility is the standard in a tax haven; even if a low profile is the exception anywhere else. Because there are only two ways to totally erase taxes and tax collectors from one's life without erasing life itself (poverty or citizenship in a no-tax haven) and you do not choose either alternative, the best of a bad situation is this: *Always keep on safe ground while taking advantage of the very substantial tax savings legally available in foreign tax havens.* Proper handling of your affairs will very probably result in a peaceful, enjoyable business that gives you much greater financial rewards than the same business registered in your home country. If through carelessness or bad luck you run afoul of the tax man, it will be a comfortable feeling to have the law on your side, even technically. He might still give you a lot of static, even take money away from you. But at least he cannot have you prosecuted or fined.

Getting back to our friend Tony, how can he blend into the landscape in ways other than what we have mentioned? To avoid problems, first we have to define them. His accumulation of profits could have been one problem if his business had been some kind of investment instead of manufacturing. Until 1962 a foreign based corporation owned by U.S. citizens could accumulate profits from any kind of foreign or U.S. sources with impunity, paying taxes only when the profits were brought to the U.S. or the corporation liquidated. That bothered the so-called "liberal" Congressmen, however, who voted restrictions on such activities. The restrictions involved several classifications of business activity, definitions of ownership, and tax penalties. They were aimed primarily at so-called "passive" income, the kind such as interest, dividends, royalties, and capital gains that accrue primarily through the mere ownership of invested capital and not from one's own labor. But they also identified other income as taxable if it resulted from transactions between related persons. Services and sales income fit this category, and it would be the related persons clause, if any, that would provide a basis for challenging Tony's tax exemption on sales profits between Amore and Groom, Ltd. There would be little question about the IRS position if Groom were merely a conduit to Tony for avoiding profits in high-tax jurisdictions. But if Tony can show evidence of a legitimate business operation at Groom and no connection to Tony, the decision turns on a matter of interpretation. And even though we cannot predict horse races or tax decisions, at worst Tony would probably not have to worry about tax evasion charges under these circumstances. There are ways not covered by the new restrictions in which Tony can avoid taxes with even less concern about challenges. *There can be no guarantee for anyone against tax challenges, remember, and no guarantee that the tax man will honor a deduction or exemption just because the tax code clearly says he will.* But if the tax office ever does look over Tony's tax return, the likelihood of a challenge will be greatly *reduced* if he takes into account the matters discussed in Chapter 1, and if the "attribution" rules cannot be successfully applied to him.

The purpose of the limited ownership is to avoid becoming a Controlled Foreign Corporation, a Foreign Personal Holding Company, or a Foreign Investment Company. For all three, one definition is that ownership is controlled by one or more U.S. citizens. Keep the ownership to half or less and you do not qualify for any of the three classifications or the taxes that IRS requires them to pay on company earnings, provided, of course, that the IRS cannot show that you have actual or constructive control over either type of company.

A company gains FIC status if it is more than 50 per cent U.S.-owned, or if it is registered under the Investment Company Act of 1940 (as amended), either as a management company or as a unit investment trust.

There is also a classification known as Personal Holding Company. Regardless of any split in ownership nationality, a company gains this unfortunate identity if five or fewer persons own a majority, and if 60 per cent or more of its total earnings come from interest, dividends, and other passive income from United States sources and/or from related-person sales or service in the U.S. If the company earnings are not distributed, the company is taxed 70 per cent on that income. It is a tax, furthermore, that is levied *in addition to* other taxes that may apply.

Tony might as well keep all his business at home as to pay that kind of tax, but he doesn't have to do either. He can avoid the yearly taxes required by this classification by making sure that the foreign corporation's stock during the last half of its taxable year is owned by non-resident aliens, whether directly or indirectly, through foreign trusts, foreign estates, foreign partnerships, or other foreign corporations. But note: all beneficiaries, partners, or shareholders must be non-resident aliens, and none of the income can be from personal service contracts. Also, a parent corporation deriving all its income from dividends from its wholly owned subsidiary is considered a "personal holding company," if the parent directs the activities of the subsidiary.

In case you are wondering about taxes on the accumulation of earnings, now would be a good time to discuss that. For U.S. tax purposes the accumulation of earnings in a foreign-based corporation gets the same treatment as for a U.S. corporation. Internal Revenue will allow a corporation a reasonable accumulation as necessary to carrying on its business. Beyond that is a $150,000 credit against taxable accumulations each year. *Only* if corporate earnings are accumulated for the purpose of avoiding tax on the shareholders does this tax apply. And only earnings accumulations from U.S. sources can be charged against this figure, and if *any* shareholders are: (a) citizens or residents of the U.S., or (b) non-resident alien individuals subject to U.S. tax, or (c) foreign corporations where a shareholder is an entity which would be subject to the tax if the income were distributed.

One thing Tony Barbier discovered in checking out his options was that threading one's way through the tax restrictions was a little more complicated than scientifically spreading his bets on the fourth race at Aqueduct. An item that surprised him a little, however, was trusts. He had always thought of trusts as the epitome of complications, but he found that some of their features were simpler than their corporate counterparts. Most notable in this regard was taxes.

First of all, he learned that a foreign trust is a "non-resident alien individual" for U.S. tax purposes, and has some advantages over a corporation:

— It must file an information return (Form 3520), but *might* not have to file an income tax return, depending upon the nature of the income.

— It is not taxed on any foreign-source income, regardless of the kind of income. This means it is not taxed on passive-type income as corporations are, although it is taxed 30 per cent on passive-type income from U.S. sources, unless its foreign base has a tax treaty with the U.S. that reduces the percentage. A foreign trust created by a U.S. person, if it has a U.S. beneficiary, is classified as a "grantor" trust. He will be taxable on all of the foreign trust's income, including income from a foreign source.

— If his stock in Amore or Groom, Ltd., is held by a trust, the stock is not probated with his estate on his death as it would be if he held the stock. And if based in the right country, it will pay no estate taxes.

Incidentally, one way of reducing taxes on the distribution of dividends is to have them paid regularly to minors or retired persons, whose lack of taxable income precludes perhaps even the lowest tax bracket. Of course, this cannot be a "sham transaction" whereby the money earner gets all the money. Another is to locate the trust in a country whose tax treaty with the U.S. reduces the tax on dividends.

The mechanics and rules in setting up a foreign-based trust are about the same as for a domestic trust. A bank, trust company, law firm, or individual is selected to act as trustee. For several good reasons, an individual is not the best choice; but if there is someone you especially trust to look after your interests, you can always name him as co-trustee. But be careful here. Your trustee may not be present in the U.S. more than 182 days in any year. Whether a co-trustee U.S. resident would compromise your foreign status if the principal trustee was permanently foreign is questionable, and it is best to be safe. The base of the trust, as well as the location of the trustee, should be in a common-law country such as Cayman Islands,

Hong Kong, Bahamas, or any of English heredity, and it should be a country that imposes no taxes. (Hong Kong takes up to 15 per cent of any trust assets located in Hong Kong, but the assets can be kept elsewhere.)

To avoid probate on the grantor's death, the trust will be an *inter vivos* or living trust, like most foreign trusts. There is no point in getting the trust fund entangled with probate by setting it up as a testamentary trust.

To keep it free of U.S. taxes, you have to remove yourself and your spouse meticulously from any control or beneficiary status. Thus, your trust must be an irrevocable trust. It should not even hold insurance on the grantor's life or his wife's. You can add to its fund, but you cannot revoke any gifts already made to it.

What about the assets—should they be held by the foreign bank or trust company? Will holding them in the States jeopardize anything? First of all, you would not place them in any country that taxed the assets. This includes Hong Kong because of its estate tax on trust assets held in Hong Kong. In second place, some of the assets might not be movable. For example, suppose Tony makes a gift of his house to the trust. (That's one way to avoid paying capital gains tax on the big house when the children leave and you and your wife move into a resort cottage.) Or what if he gives something fragile or something he wants to look at or use now and then, such as his gun collection? On the other hand, some experts will say that you make a stronger case for avoiding U.S. estate taxes if *everything* is out of the grantor's proximity and under the care and control of a foreign trustee and government.

Finally, there is the matter of economic and political stability. You want your assets located in the safest jurisdiction. Some persons say that means the United States, because some local police chief or army officer can take over the government of a small foreign island nation and expropriate all foreign assets. Others say that there is a trend against private ownership of property in the U.S., that a future socialist government might grab it all; whereas, the trend is going in favor of private ownership in a number of countries, including the ones we have been talking about. Maybe the answer is to spread it around. Certainly if the grantor sees a threat coming, he can, through a Memorandum of Wishes, suggest his trustee move the assets to a safer location. You can also add a safeguard to your trust instrument called a Cuba Clause. Since the Castro takeover in Cuba, many trusts have been set up with instructions about where to move the trust (having checked that out first) and what conditions would trigger automatic removal. We are talking mainly about the *situs*, or location, of course. Any efficient takeover will close all banks and other institutions to prevent the flight of assets. So your treasure in such a location would be in serious jeopardy, at least during the crisis.

On the subject of capital gains and the advantages of a foreign trust Tony wonders why he couldn't be a *beneficiary* of a trust and enjoy some of his investment. He loves his family, of course, and wants the trust he sets up for them after his death to stay safe, free and clear of anything else he does. But maybe through another trust he could do some things he couldn't do through a corporation. A grantor can also be a beneficiary under the laws of some tax havens, although the U.S. tax law sometimes does not give the treatment accorded to beneficiaries who are also grantors whom the IRS holds have not "really" ceased to be owners of the trust property. The IRS can be very arbitrary at times, however, and it might simply ignore the claims of any living trust that names the grantor as beneficiary. The grantor, of course, could be some foriegn "person," such as a corporation named Amore or another named Groom, Ltd. That might not accomplish anything except to get the IRS on the trail of the corporations. *Otherwise, it at least would not be so obvious as Tony's setting up a trust for himself.* Naturally, he will have to pay a second annual fee that will depend on the size of the fund—probably another $250 to $1,000 a year. One firm, The Derek H.M. Price & Company, in the Cayman Islands charges no fixed annual fee on an ordinary trust. A 1% per annum charge is assessed on assets with a 1% withdrawal fee. This means the fees are low when the amount of money in the trust is small.

To make a point, though, let's say that Tony wants to arrange a trust to benefit him in his retirement. Because he cannot build in all the hands-off features that will protect his family's trust against taxes, he expects to get hit when his trust distributes its assets. But he would like it to be more like a nick than a blow. Except for dividends and capital gains on the appreciation of U.S. stocks, his trust would ideally not have to be concerned about passive income, Sub-part F income, U.S. versus foreign control, and other little headaches. And while he is pursuing other matters, his trust is compounding equity on top of equity with nothing taken away for taxes.

Where would the equity come from? He could, of course, fund it with cash as a starter. Or he could start it with a gift of something substantial. (We will get back to the matter of taxes on the gifts and how people avoid them.) He could then go cautiously and simply have his trust bank it in the U.S. at the highest long-term interest. (Remember, foreigners can have tax-free savings accounts in the U.S.) If he only started with $10,000 and got just 8 per cent simple interest compounded yearly, by his chosen retirement age in eighteen years it would amount to about $40,000. As we have observed, however, Tony is a guy with initiative, and he does not consider that a good investment. Not when his trust in Hong Kong (or Cayman) can buy Asia Currency Units paying 12 per cent or get interest from Mexican banks paying as high as 16 per cent. Not when he can double his investment every two or three years by building resort cottages in the Canary Islands, or even by purchasing acreage in the U.S. and watching its value grow like bamboo.

You might be wondering why anyone would go to the extent of setting up a foreign retirement trust if he qualifies for the new Individual Retirement Account just enacted for U.S. workers not covered by company pension plans. After all, the earnings from your investments in an IRA accumulate tax free, and the contributions or investments are deductible from income tax. As a matter of fact, Tony can start an IRA for himself, because he is self-employed. Depending on his tax bracket, it could be an excellent investment, mainly because of its tax benefits. The trouble with it is that Tony is allowed to contribute a maximum of just $1,500 a year (even if they raise the ceiling, it will still be small), and he cannot invest in what he wants—specifically, investments that pay much more than any IRA. Nevertheless, it could be a wise addition to his investment portfolio, something conservative for the mental comfort it might give him in addition to maybe an additional $50,000 when he retires. Also as far as what Tony can do in the U.S., he can set up a corporation, say in

Delaware, and put in up to the lesser of $7,500 or 15% of his "earned" income a year tax free in his own profit sharing or pension plan. This can give him $150,000 or more at retirement, depending upon his age at the time of the creation of the IRA vehicle.

Now us turn to the matter of endowing the trust fund or shipping any kind of equity out of the country or bringing it back into the country. At the present time, the lack of restrictions on the movement of dollars across the border is one of the few beacons of light in the gloom of U.S. tax policy. And that benefit might not last long.

Ironically, with the U.S. balance-of-payments problems, it is easier to ship money out than to bring it in legally without doling out taxes. We mentioned the gift-tax exemptions that can be used in creating a trust. You can make cash contributions to a corporation without paying a gift tax. And in any event, you do not have to declare anything that is not more than $5,000 a transaction going in either direction.

We also mentioned lending your corporation money to help get it started. And the ratio of loan to paid-for shares can be much more liberal for a foreign corporation than for a domestic one, depending, of course, on the laws of your tax haven country. After your corporation has built sufficiently on your loan to provide its own operating capital and reserve, you repatriate your money along with modest interest your corporation pays you. This makes the loan legitimate and saves you and the corporation from paying taxes on the money. (You should pay taxes on the interest portion.) When donating a gift to your trust, obviously it will benefit you to have it evaluated at the lowest possible figure. You are penalized for the gift, remember, and not for the capital gain, or appreciation, of the gift after you give it. Money is also transferred to and from trusts and corporations by installment sales, but the IRS might take issue with this method if the sales are not made at "arm's length" (are prearranged).

And then there is the cash-transfer method of getting a cashier's or certified check payable to yourself, which you endorse "deposit to my account only" and mail to your agent or bank in your tax haven. The amount is credited to your foreign account, but there is nothing to show this when the certified check reaches the U.S. clearing house and is microfilmed. It shows that the amount was paid to you by a

U.S. bank. Any cancellation by the foreign bank, if readable at all, is on the back which is usually not microfilmed. This method, of course works in one direction only.

We dislike closing this chapter on a hurried note or one of pessimism about a near-future clampdown on foreign trusts. But we do feel it is our duty to tell you about legislation enacted by the Tax Revision Act (TRA) of 1976. The tax laws regarding trusts were amended so that:

—The grantor of any foreign trust having U.S. beneficiaries will be taxed on its assets during his lifetime: he is treated as the owner.

—If somehow the grantor escapes taxation, the beneficiaries are taxed for every year of accumulation, plus 6 per cent annual interest that will not be deductible.

—The excise tax on the transfer of appreciated U.S. securities has increased from 27.5 per cent to 35 per cent, and the coverage has been expanded to include all property—not just securities, and the tax applies to all deferred recognition sales or exchanges.

Undoubtedly, the persons behind this are of the type who believe they can channel that foreign investment into higher FICA deductions for higher and higher social security payments. And then finally everyone will be raised and lowered to the same even level and we will have true equality in a socialist Utopia. Those persons should see what income levels are starting to invest through tax havens. Then they would realize that it is not the wealthy alone who are working to escape harsh taxes and tax laws. Increasingly, it is the little guy they claim to be helping.

Even with the legislation just described, the ingenuity of honest people will find a solution. Perhaps it will be somewhere in the clauses that deal with the nationality of trusts, donors, and beneficiaries. Right now, for example, the creation of a foreign trust or the making of gifts to a foreign trust must be reported only when the grantor or donor is a U.S. person. If a foreign trust is created by a foreign-based corporation, which is not a U.S. person, then technically, no report is required. And if the beneficiary were a foreign-based corporation—offically an alien—and not a U.S. person, who knows what might be worked out with bearer shares and beneficiaries?

6 The Special Significance Of Multi-Nationality

So far, we have limited our discussion pretty much to the Cayman Islands. We said earlier that we think it is one of the best tax havens but surely not the only one worth using. Our friend, Tony, in fact used the Bahamas to good effect in order to get maximum benefit from Cayman. Also, in dealing from a foreign base, he avoided acquiring a Resident status in either the Caymans or the Bahamas. This is no great problem except that you are required to deal in the local currency when conducting more than incidental business locally. Then you have to get permission from Exchange Control to convert the local money to any other kind for dealing offshore. A Non-resident status allows you to keep your money in U.S. dollars or anything else you wish. You then avoid the time delays and inconvenience of exchanging currencies and possible losses from currency fluctuations in the market. In Tony's case he also benefited from the Bahamas' larger population, closer proximity to raw materials in the U.S., and the absence of a company-branch registration fee, an item he would have had to pay the Cayman government if he had worked it in reverse.

The greatest benefits come from the flexibility of using several havens to obtain the best features of each. A multinational operation can also provide greater privacy and security against political instability. Whether we are talking about privacy, security, or flexibility, we are talking about putting your eggs in several baskets. Most of us have learned the hard lesson of carrying all our eggs in one basket.

For privacy, the more closed doors you can put between yourself and any snoopers, the more inaccessible you will be. Tycoons and bureaucrats build a labyrinth of outer offices between their private office and pestiferous persons. Although that will not be the main reason for a multinational business structure, it is an added benefit.

For security, multinationality means a dispersed target. No gopher in its right mind would have a burrow with just one exit; no sane squirrel would hide all its acorns in one cache. Even humans have learned to scatter their factories and gun emplacements during wartime. Barring a globular calamity, the financial survivors of any local or regional upheavals will be the farsighted souls who tucked it away in a number of places. That, too, is a tertiary benefit, although it could be your salvation at some future date.

The principal inducement for most persons at the present time is the much greater range of opportunities open to them through the use of several countries. We have already touched on various ways that substantial tax benefits attach to persons using the Cayman Islands, the Bahamas, and the United States. We could have used other countries for some of our examples.

Tony Barbiere, for instance, could have made the wildly popular blue jeans in Ireland and sold them tax free to the European Common Market or even to eastern Europe where they are not only popular but scarce as well. Or he could have made cowboy hats or baseball bats in Hong Kong for the American-fads market in Japan.

Hong Kong, with its still inexpensive and dexterous hand labor, would be a good location also for manufacturing umbrellas for the proper gentlemen of Australia and New Zealand. Admittedly, setting up a manufacturing operation so far from home could pose some problems. But there is nothing in the location of Hong Kong that would interfere with the basing of a corporation or trust there to conduct business closer to home. This could include a service business in Canada, Mexico, the U.S., or elsewhere; real estate investment wherever the opportunities appear to be; or buying and selling someone else's products. The no-tax havens would obviously be best for these kinds of businesses.

As for investing in U.S. corporations or buying land in the U.S., a tax haven having low taxes and a treaty with the United States would be best. The treaties go with the taxes, and the treaties cover such things as taxes on dividends, interest, real estate, and sales of manufactured goods. To profit from those ventures, therefore, you need a corporation based in the British Virgin Islands, Antigua, Barbados, or Netherlands Antilles. An Antigua-based corporation, we cited, pays only about 17 per cent instead of the 30 per cent tax that a Cayman or Bermuda, Bahamas, Turks, and Caicos, on the other hand, impose no taxes for activities of their corporations and trusts. (U.S. shareholders of their corporations and trusts would pay the 30 per cent tax on the dividends of U.S. corporations.) A Netherlands Antilles holding company pays 24 per cent instead of the regular 30 per cent on interest from U.S. sources. By interest, we mean something like a mortgage on U.S. property; savings-account interest is tax free to any foreign person. Another possible advantage to having a Netherlands Antilles corporation is tax-free profits on the sale of goods in the U.S. This would be possible, though, only if the corporation maintained no fixed place of business in the U.S.

We should dwell a moment on this matter of selling goods in the U.S. through a foreign-based corporation. If you sell through agents or distributors and not from your own sales office or warehouse, you have no fixed place of business in the U.S. for the corporation. If you sell by mail the same situation would apply. Just how important a treaty is between the U.S. and the base country for your corporation is open to question. We used the example of the Netherlands Antilles because of its treaty with the U.S. But could you sell tax-free in the U.S. from a corporation based in the Cayman Islands or the Bahamas, which have no tax treaties with the U.S.? One wonders, first of all, how the tax people would even notice and, if they noticed, how they could pin it on the U.S. owners of such a corporation when they don't know who the owners are. Secondly, there is another out for the Cayman-based corporation: If it transfers title to the goods outside the U.S. and the new owners of the goods are independent brokers, the sales profits should be tax-free to U.S. shareholders. Brokers, of course, don't pay for goods when they take possession of them or place an order for them. So unless you made some kind of special arrangement with the broker, you would be surrendering title to the goods somewhat in advance of getting paid for them.

What it all adds up to is a corporation in the Cayman Islands for its no-tax benefits in offshore activities such as sales or investments; a corporation in Antigua for investments in income-producing U.S. corporation shares; and a corporation in the Netherlands Antilles to hold stock in the other two corporations, thereby as a holding company qualifying for its tax benefits, provided the corporation is properly structured and its tie to U.S. taxpayers is not clear. Individually, each corporation could realize some of those benefits. But by owning all three, a person could benefit from them all.

One other interesting benefit from the Netherlands Antilles-U.S. treaty concerns developed real estate investment in the U.S. We already said that a foreign corporation could buy, hold, and sell unimproved U.S. real estate without paying a capital gains tax. You disqualify yourself, however, if you as much as sink a well on the property.

But through the tax treaty your Netherlands Antilles corporation could buy a shopping center or an apartment building in the U.S. and enjoy advantages that U.S. citizens could not. The treaty allows the corporation to elect on an annual basis to be considered "engaged in trade or business within the United States." Here is the point: As a foreign corporation earning income from U.S. property, the tax penalty would be a straight 30 per cent with no deductions. By electing to be considered "doing business," the corporation pays the usual U.S. taxes on net income. The rate is higher than 30 per cent, but now the corporation can take depreciation and deductions for mortgage interest and taxes. In the early stages of such an investment, the heavy deductions can entirely cancel the taxes; and any net losses can be carried forward to later years to help offset taxes. Finally, when taxes start rising because of reduced deductions, the corporation can deliberately fail to elect "doing business" status, then sell out. At this juncture it has reverted to its regular foreign-person status, and consequently any capital gain on sale of the property is immune to U.S. capital gains tax.

As you can see, much of the multinational activities described here depend on the tax treaties that exist among nations, and especially between certain nations and the United States. These treaties do offer benefits, as you can see; but we should remind you once again that they can be a mixed blessing. The treaties stipulate that each country will provide the other with information if requested, and that could mean information on your corporation or trust. Maybe that is all right, but maybe it is not. The information provided would probably only consist of your annual report containing the names of your nominee shareholders and directors; and in most instances if more information is requested, the tax haven will reply that it is all they require of their corporations and therefore all they have.

On balance, multinationality of business operations can provide all the advantages we cited at the beginning of this chapter.

Finally in the realm of multinationality, let us return to a point we made briefly earlier in the book. And that is the point about U.S. citizens earning money in foreign countries without having to pay taxes on it. To translate Section 911 of the Internal Revenue Code: You can work for a salary or for fees anywhere in the world outside the United States, its Territories and Possessions, and pay no taxes to the U.S. on the income, provided that the income source is not related to any U.S. business. It must be compensation for your labor and not income from capital investment. And the maximum you can earn without paying U.S. income tax is, in most cases, $15,000 a year. You will pay any income tax to the country in which you are working, and in a few countries that could mean a bigger tax than the U.S. citizen would pay at home. But if the employment occurred in any of the countries we have been talking about in this book, you would pay little or nothing.

You have to meet one of two tests in order to qualify. One is the Bona Fide Residence Test. This test requires you to be a real resident of a foreign country for an uninterrupted period of time spanning an entire taxable year. This doesn't mean that you can't set foot on U.S. soil during that time, but since there are no hard rules covering this test, the less you are in the U.S., the better your chances of qualifying. And you must be more than a transient resident, hopping back and forth and from place to place. Anything such as long-term leases, driver's permit, club memberships, and so forth, that will document your status as a legitimate resident of a foreign country will improve your chances. The other test is the Physical Presence Test. This test says you must be present in some foreign country for at least 510 full days, or about 17 months, during any period of 18 consecutive months.

Can your U.S. corporation hire you to work in, say, the Cayman Islands for Cayman-source income and escape taxation? Not if you own or partially own the company and a substantial share of its income is from capital investment. Then only 30 per cent of your share of the company's income can be exempted under this rule. Of course, if your company is an Ordinary Resident company in Cayman paying you a salary from non-U.S. source income, you could. At least, until some faction engineers a deletion of this feature from the Code.

7 The Importance of Keeping Informed

One of our purposes in writing this book was to simplify the understanding of a subject that has been all too complicated for the understanding of most persons. We have not, and of course could not, simplify the facts as they exist. But we have put them into what we think are common-enough terms for persons not holding law degrees to appreciate. Lawyers get so used to communicating in their quaint idiom they forget that the great big world out there speaks a different language. More often than being impressed by the professional jargon, people are annoyed. And that is unfortunate, because their annoyance drives them to more pleasant occupations and away from matters that could benefit them if they understood them. Understanding by laymen takes nothing away from the lawyer, and in fact is of benefit, for in most instances the annoyed person will simply forget the whole thing if he has a choice.

We don't want that to happen to persons who might otherwise reap real rewards from the use of tax havens. Hence this book. As far as we know, the book contains the latest developments on the tax-haven scene. Changes occur frequently, however, and there will be changes after the book's publication. As fast as they happen, fortunately, the growing number of experts in this field of activity record the facts and distribute them to all interested parties. Included in this army are the persons with whom you will ultimately deal in the organizing of your foreign entity. Also, revised and updated editions of this book will be published when appropriate.

You may, therefore, with confidence use the forms provided in this book as the first step in forming your company or trust. You can and should, at the time you send them in, review the options and requirements with your foreign correspondent. He will be glad to correspond with you, because it is strictly in his interest to treat you kindly and have you fully informed.

None of us like ugly surprises, especially the kind that cost us money. So where our money is concerned, it pays to keep alert. If you haven't already discovered it, you can be sure that investment makes one very knowledgeable on the subject without even trying. Subjects that use to bore you to yawns will suddenly become very stimulating. News that used to pass you totally unnoticed will now jump out at you. You will even find yourself understanding some of what the lawyers and accountants are talking about. And the more you learn, the more interesting the whole subject will become, leading to a sharper business sense in you, greater rewards, and more stimulation.

The information you will need is surprisingly available. The most important even appears in the daily newspapers. Other sources are the popular news magazines, newsletters, business publications in great variety. And if you want to be sure you get all pertinent up-to-date news, you can subscribe to any of several tax-haven reports that are published regularly. You can get information on this from your tax-haven agent also, as well as from sources closer to home (libraries, private tax consultants, editors of financial and business publications, and so forth).

Whatever changes occur, however, we feel certain that there will always be tax havens and ways to use them, even for the American taxpayer. In fact, it is the very tightening of the rules by U.S. tax authorities and their advocates in Congress that will cause the walls to crack and crumble. We reiterate that nothing can work unless the people affected by it are in favor of it. The harsher the rules become, the heavier the tax burden, the faster will grow the flow of American investment toward the tax havens. Only when sanity returns to government spending and taxation will the flow recede and voluntary support re-establish the equilibium.

In the meantime should you desire the financial benefits available to you, we urge you to keep informed.

8 Two Tax Havens Of Special Merit

There are in the world at present more than thirty no-tax or low-tax havens. A hundred years ago virtually all nations were tax havens in the sense that their taxes were infinitesimal compared to the taxes of most nations today. In the next decade there will be more tax-haven countries than there are now. In a way, the supply of tax havens is like the supply of beef: Both rise with demand for them and diminish with a falling-off in demand. Tax havens will prosper until calamitously shrinking revenue in high-tax nations and a subsequent drop in tax rates bring investment back to their shores. Then the specialty tax-haven business will shrivel. This cycle has been repeated thoughtout human history.

What brings on the calamitous shrinking of revenues? It has been caused by capital flight, economic stagnation and depression, and revolution in government. Often these causes are interrelated. One fact appears certain and fixed: Man never learns from his mistakes so is doomed to repeat them. We can read about the fall of Rome, the French and American revolutions, and evidently fail to see the connection. Men fled to America to escape English taxes, then revolted and chased the British out when the king's taxes followed them to their haven. Now America is imposing the same burden on itself that it once fought to escape, and now its citizens are beginning once again to flee. So are the citizens of other high-tax nations. The tax-haven business is entering a boom period.

In competing with one another for this growth market, the havens offer a variety of inducements to the flight capital. These inducements make a choice or choices somewhat difficult, although if the investor has pretty well in mind what he wants to do, the choices narrow. As we and others have said, there is no one best tax haven for all persons. If there were, there would be only one tax haven. While acknowledging the merits of others, we feel that the net benefits of two generally give them an edge, but for specific reasons. These two are the Cayman Islands and Hong Kong. Let us take them one at a time and explain why.

Cayman Islands

This is a politically and economically stable country. It has enjoyed such security and tranquility since its first colonization by the British some three hundred years ago. It remains by choice a Crown Colony and hereby enjoys the combined benefits of local government and British resources. Its citizens could have become totally independent in 1962 when Jamaica separated from Great Britain. Cayman at the time was a dependency of Jamacia, and both were within the British Empire. Cayman, however, applied the time-honored rule that you don't change a winning combination. Its citizens could not see how things could be any better than they were. And their opting for the status quo demonstrates as much as anything else that the politico-economic situation there is eminently satisfactory and sound.

Its location, five hundred miles due south of Miami and about equidistant from North, South, and Central America, places it in a strategic position for commercial transactions. We have said that location and distance are no practical problem for businesses involving only written and verbal communication. Manufacturing and sales, however, do require consideration of proximity to raw materials and markets. Yet even in this instance, remember that your manufacturing operation can be located near your source of supply, or your markets and your company base can be anywhere else.

Another unusual benefit available in the Cayman Islands (otherwise available only in Bermuda, Gibraltar, and New Hebrides) is the Exempted form of company, which among other features provides tighter secrecy and a guarantee against future taxes. Even an Ordinary company enjoys privacy and freedom from taxes, which condition will likely prevail indefinitely with or without guarantees.

Rather unusual also are bearer shares, which can be issued by exempt companies. By these you can transfer the ownership of your company and transfer it back again by simply handling the shares certificate to someone else and having him hand it back to you.

One other point deserves reiteration: Cayman has strong secrecy laws. A number of countries have such laws on the books, but some countries do not enforce them. Cayman, however, is very serious about the matter because everyone agrees that it is the key to their future. Any violators will be severely punished by heavy fines and imprisonment. Since the probability of getting caught is high, and the total punishment will be greater than any reward, there is virtually no likelihood of any leak.

Facilities. The Cayman Islands' British heritage is, if anything, growing in significance as Cayman positions itself to compete in the expanding tax-haven market. Besides the military support that protects the local government against any possible insurrection or invasion, the British influence is evident in the English talent for organization, administration, and law. The Cayman business entities are as sophisticated as you will find, the facilities of modern intercourse as efficient as required for conducting whatever kind of enterprise. The English common law provides the only real basis for the establishment of a trust, this making the Cayman Islands equal in this respect to any other common-law country and superior to any civil-law country. As for communication, remember that the basis of all communication is language, and that the universal language of business and technology is English, the only language spoken in the Cayman Islands except for that of a few Spanish-speaking immigrants. The technical aspects of communication, including transportation, are present in virtually every medium. These include worldwide telephone, telegraph and telex service, sea and air transportation on regular schedules. One medium still absent but anticipated is television, although there are some persons who would count the absence a blessing. Radio broadcasts are received from the Cayman Government station and from the U.S., Jamaica, and Latin America.

Services. In addition to modern police, fire, medical and dental facilities, and skilled professional personnel for the local population, Cayman is so endowed with business and financial services as to appear top-heavy in this department. This is particularly true in the case of banks and trust companies, although there are also more accounting and law firms than you would expect to find for a population of only sixteen thousand. Normally, you would find about three banks for that number of persons. The Cayman Islands are pushing three *hundred*. We must quickly add, however, that the great majority of them are not licensed to do business in the Islands. They are an effect and also a cause of the tax-haven phenomenon, and specifically of the Cayman benevolence toward business and revulsion toward taxes. They operate either as captive banking operations of foreign corporations or as commercial banks providing services for foreign corporations and individuals. These are the banks operating under a "B" license; and whether they are allowed to provide business for any source outside Cayman or are limited to servicing one or several specific companies is determined by a Restricted or Unrestricted subclassification. A bank's annual fee depends on its classification. The banks classified as "A" can provide services for anyone in or out of the Cayman Islands. You would recognize names from all over the world and from many of the United States in the "B" list, but because it is so long we will list below the "A" banks to let you see some of the financial powers that are licensed there:

American Express International Banking Corporation
Arawak Trust Company (Cayman) Limited
Bank of America National Trust & Savings Associations
Bank of America Trust & Banking Corporation (Cayman) Ltd.
Bank of Credit & Commerce International (Overseas) Ltd.
Bank of Virginia (Grand Cayman) Limited
Barclays Bank International Limited
Barclays Finance Corporation of the Cayman Islands Limited
Canadian Imperial Bank of Commerce
Canadian Imperial Bank of Commerce Trust
    Company (Cayman) Limited
Caribbean Bank (Cayman) Limited
Cayman International Trust Company Limited
Cayman National Bank and Trust Company Ltd.
Chase Manhattan Trust Cayman Ltd.
Cititrust (Cayman) Limited

Dow Banking (Overseas) Ltd.
European-American Bank and Trust Company
First Cayman Bank, Ltd.
First Cayman Trust Company, Ltd.
Guinness Mahon Cayman Trust Limited
J. Henry Schroeder Bank & Trust Co.
LBI Bank and Trust Company (Cayman) Limited
Ray West Trust Corporation (Cayman) Limited
Schroeder Cayman Bank & Trust Company, Ltd.
Swiss Bank and Trust Corporation Limited
The Bank of Nova Scotia
The Bank of Nova Scotia Trust Company (Cayman) Limited
The Chase Manhattan Bank
The Royal Bank of Canada
The Royal Bank of Canada International Limited

A choice of bank or trust company from such a list might bewilder the reader who is personally unfamiliar with any of them, so let us reassure you. You could undoubtedly throw a dart at the list and make a good choice based on soundness. But we would rather make two suggestions to help you. First, even though there is a temptation to work with a bank that is headquartered in your city or country, this could be exactly the wrong choice. We say that because, for example, U.S. Internal Revenue might successfully require a U.S. bank to supply information from one of its branches or subsidiaries in your tax haven. Furthermore, remember our warning about jeopardizing the status of your foreign trust if the IRS should assert that the trustee is a U.S. resident because it is headquartered in the U.S. For these reasons, then, we believe that you should select either a Cayman bank or one that does not have a branch in your own country. A wise choice might be the Cayman branch of a Swiss bank. Then if any kind of trouble developed in the Cayman Islands, you could more easily transfer your assets to a safe location. The second suggestion we make is to let your Cayman agent recommend a bank for you. After all, he knows the banks and the bankers and probably favors one or several. If his recommendation agrees with your security and privacy wishes, you might as well accept it. Incidentally, he can take care of the details in opening an account for your company.

This is as good a place as any, in fact, to give you the name and address of a Cayman agent who can act as advisor, representative, and manager of your tax haven affairs. We are not saying that this is the only company who can do the job for you. We happen to know this firm well enough to recommend their services without any reservations. Nevertheless, any agent will handle your interests to best effect if you communicate to him your special preferences, dislikes, inclinations, goals, and objectives. You should also check his course against your own knowledge so that you can rest confident at all times that your business is going the way you want it to.

> International Management Services Ltd.
> P.O. Box 61
> Grand Cayman
> Cayman Islands
> British West Indies
> (Phone: 9-4244)

Taxes. Are you ready? We are now going to list all the important taxes paid by Caymanians once a year:

1. Head tax, males only, ages 18 to 59 $10.00
2. Cayman-registered vessels $50.00 minimum
3. Motorboats up to 30 h.p. $10.00
4. Bicycles $ 2.00

That's it. There used to be a few other incidental taxes that were abolished in 1971 as too onerous. One might even say that the above so-called taxes are really fees, so there really are no direct taxes at all and certainly none for nonresidents. Nevertheless, Americans should remember that those are Cayman Island dollars which are worth $1.20 in American money. So a Caymanian male in his prime, owning a four-ton cruiser, a catamaran, and a bicycle, will pay $4.20 a year in "taxes," which is about $5.00 in U.S. dollars. There are sundry other charges, such as on motor vehicle registrations, driver's licenses, and a $2.40 tax on flight departures.

How can a modern society get along without any income taxes on individuals or corporations, without capital gains taxes, property taxes, sales taxes, estate and inheritance taxes, or death duties? They function quite well on the import and stamp duties, company registration fees, and the general prosperity engendered by the infusion of foreign capital from investments and tourism. Also, their operating expenses are low. They have little need for welfare or unemployment compensation. The crime rate is almost nonexistent. They have no congestion or pollution problems. They need no defense budget. And they have very little government overhead because they have very little government or need for it. They do not believe that the government should provide every creature need. Without a heavy tax burden, the people can provide for themselves. Finally, they do not engage regularly in massive deficit spending.

Requirements for starting and running a Cayman Island Company.

1. Decide whether yours will be an **Ordinary** or **Exempt** Company. An **Ordinary** company cost less to start and run; nominee directors allowed; beneficial owners' identity not required on annual returns; bearer shares not permitted, par value shares required; "Limited" or "Ltd." must be part of name.

   Both **Ordinary** and **Exempt** companies are categorized as *resident* or *non-resident* which is an exchange control point. If a corporation is classified as non-resident, which is the classification given to virtually all corporations formed by non-Caymanians, all business must be done in foreign currency (currency other than Cayman dollars). This is easy to do, just a technical point. No land in the Caymans can be owned, nor can a business be operated there without special permission which can often be obtained, but it is better to have a resident company for that purpose.

   Government fees for non-resident **Ordinary** are higher than for resident **Ordinary** companies. This is because Cayman businessmen use resident **Ordinary** companies and the government wishes to keep the fees lower for them.

   An **Exempt** company costs more to start and run; nominees allowed, beneficial owners' or actual shareholders' identities not required on annual returns; bearer shares and no-par value shares permitted; "Limited" not required in name; twenty-year guarantee of no taxes.

The decision must be made before filing application; once registered, the company cannot change from one status to the other.

2. Decide whether you will have *nominee directors*. They give you privacy but cost extra.

3. *Memorandum of Association.* Your agent can draw this up for you, based on information you send him on your application form and on any supplemental information you might add following correspondence with him.

> The memorandum will contain:
>
> a. name of the company.
> b. address of the registered office.
> c. general purpose of the company.
> d. statement that shareholders have limited liability.
> e. amount of authorized capital, number, and par value of shares.
>
> *No minimum capital is required,* and you do not have to subscribe for or issue all the authorized capital. If your stated capital is less than U.S. $914,000, the registration and annual fees will be based on that minimum for Ordinary companies. Exempt companies are also based on a U.S. $975,000 authorized capital.

4. *Articles of Association.* These, the by-laws, are not required; but if you do not include them, the Registrar of Companies will supply a standard form, and these might not agree with your plans. You can file the Articles with the Memorandum or later. Note, however, that if filed in the beginning they need be signed by the three subscribers only; if filed later they must be signed by all shareholders. The stamp duty on the Articles is U.S. $7.32.

5. *Three subscribers* or incorporators are required, and each must agree to take one share minimum. If these are nominee subscribers and shareholders provided by your agent, you can arrange to

have them transfer ownership to you after the certificate of incorporation is issued. Anyone who is not a resident of the Cayman Islands must obtain permission from government authorities if he wishes to be a subscriber to a Memorandum or Association. This is not too difficult to obtain, but it is a tedious process and not recommended. It is much better to have Cayman resident subscribers and transfer afterwards.

An ordinary company must have three shareholders at all times. An exempt company need only have one. Therefore, if a private individual wants to have the shares all issued to him, he must have an exempt company. Otherwise he must have two shares held by someone else. Of Course, he can have, i.e., 998 shares issued to himself and one each to two other people. Moreover, the transfer of shares in the case of an exempted company is not reported to the Registrar; whereas, it is in the case of an ordinary company. Therefore, for privacy the beneficial owners of an ordinary company must continue to use nominees or trustees.

6. For an Exempt company you should probably have at least two *directors*. If they are nominee directors, you will be asked by your agent to sign a form indemnifying them from any liability connected with the operation or any bankruptcy of the company.

7. Americans, Canadians, and other nonresidents of the Cayman Islands whose companies will deal exclusively outside the Cayman Islands will need a certificate from Exchange Control granting the company *Nonresident Status*. This enables it to deal freely in any currency other than Cayman dollars. *Approved Status* is also required for the purchase of any Cayman property. However, it is expected that Exchange Control will be abandoned in whole or in part before much longer.

8. *Filing*, of *incorporating costs*. These consist mainly of the government incorporation fee and your agent's charges.

	Ordinary Co.	Exempt Co.
Government fee (inc. all disbursements	U.S. $ 520	U.S. $ 950
Agent fee (for standard memorandum and articles of incorporation)	600	600
Total:	$ 1120	$ 1550

Your check for the government fee (and your agent's) will have to accompany your Confidential Information Form when it is submitted.

9. *Annual costs.* In addition to the annual registration fee, these will include your agent's charges plus overhead costs. Your agent will charge extra for keeping minutes, and for all work done in managing your company beyond incorporation matters. For overhead we are including the large items but not such things as stationery, postage, telephone, telex, etc. All annual fees (Government and Agent's) are due in January of each year following incorporation.

	Ordinary Co.	Exempt Co.
Government registration fee	U.S. $ 260	U.S. $ 470
Registered office fee (inc. lodgement of Annual Return)	350	350
Nominee Shareholders	50	50
Nominee Directors	U.S. $ 500	U.S. $500

10. *Additional Information About Agents:*
   — The Annual Registered Office Charge includes maintenance of Registered Office, furnishing Nominee Shareholders (if required), arranging for holding of Annual General Meeting (if in Cayman Islands), arranging Statutory Annual Meeting

of Directors (Exempted Companies only), maintaining Registers and filing the Annual Return.

— These agents recommend having a minimum of two Directors and a Secretary. If provided by them, there is a charge of $100 per annum for each Director or Officer so provided. If instructed to provide all Directors and Officers, they will provide two Directors, one of whom will act as Chairman and the other as Secretary, at a flat charge of $200 per annum.

— Annual Registered Office and Directors fees are payable every twelve months commencing with the date of incorporation of the Company. Annual Government fees are payable every January, commencing the January following incorporation.

Other Services. These services include investment management, purchase and sale of securities and commodities, safe-keeping, acting as agent or transfer agent, transmission of funds, re-invoicing for sales companies, ship registration, registration of partnership and other documents, bookkeeping, mail forwarding, etc. Terms are available upon request.

11. *Other useful suggestions and information.*

Toll Calls

(first 3 min.)   Miami: $10.00   NYC: $12.00   Calif.: $14.00

— If you have some reason to do so, your company can be incorporated and recorded within twenty-four hours of submitting the memorandum.

— All correspondence with your agent should be sent *air mail*. Unlike the U.S. first-class mail that all travels the same way, your letters will go by a very slow boat if you send them just first class. That might mean six months to deliver a letter. Air mail gets there in about four days from major U.S. cities.

— When transferring money between your home bank and your agent, use certified, cashier's, or treasurer's checks or postal money orders. If the checks are made out to you, they can travel either way for deposit to your account at home or your company's account in Cayman. The fewer places your name is associated with your company, the more privacy you are likely to enjoy. Another reason is that personal checks take too long to clear in transactions between countries. Remember, too, that if the checks are $5,000 (U.S.) or smaller, they do not have to be reported.

— Your corporate seal and company records must be kept by your directors.

— Arrangements for paying bills, writing checks, making deposits, and so forth, will be decided between you and your agent. If you are not sure how to handle these matters, he can probably offer a suggestion based on his experience. You will naturally want control of disbursements from your company's bank account, but if your agent provides nominee directors, they will naturally want to retain control over all the company's assets. In fact, the law holds them responsible for such assets. Although the arrangements you make with your agent can be changed at any time (or you can change agents), you must decide whether your company is going to be controlled from Cayman (by nominee directors) or from your own home country (by yourself or your own nominees as directors).

Cost of a Trust. Your trustee's fee will depend on how active the instrument and your wishes cause him to be. This is true both of the original time and effort in drawing up the papers and the administration of the fund.

As for a regular trust, it will cost U.S. $500 plus stamp duty of approximately $50 to establish, and $250 a year administration. Most ordinary trusts are not recorded, as privacy is lost. There are no government fees for this kind of trust as opposed to an Exempt trust. We do not believe, in most cases, that the latter is worth your extra investment, which gives you a fifty-year guarantee against future taxation on both capital and income. The latter would cost at least U.S. $600 to set up and U.S. $120 a year government fee plus trustee's fee.

It should be noted that most Cayman banks, attorneys and accountants offer incorporation and trust services. All of the ones we researched charge varying fees considerably higher than the ones quoted in this chapter. Since there is such a wide range we did not include all of them. If you wish to obtain the actual fees you can do so by writing directly.

If you decide to go ahead with a Cayman corporation or trust on the basis of the information and fees described in this chapter, all that you need do is complete the simple one page form on the following page and send with your check to the agent previously mentioned. International Management Services, because of special arrangements made for readers of this book, will permit you to *deduct 20%* from the *agent portion* of the incorporation fees previously quoted. For example, to incorporate an ordinary company, cost for first year would be $900 (instead of $1,120), an exempt company $1,430 (instead of $1,550). A simple trust starts at $500 less 20%. Note: Be sure to use forms on following page in order to receive your discount. If you have any further questions, you should telephone the recommended agent.

Hong Kong

This island, lying less than a mile off the Asiatic mainland, along with an enclave on the mainland and another island adjacent to it, has been owned by Great Britain since about the middle of the last century. Hong Kong Island with the capital of Victoria and Hong Kong harbor comprise the business and commercial center of this British Crown Colony. Kowloon, number two city of the Colony, is on a mainland peninsula pointed toward Hong Kong. Althogether, with Stonecutter's Island, the British-owned part of the Colony is about 33 square miles. The Hong Kong government also controls another 365 square miles leased from China until mid-1997.

There are about four million residents of Hong Kong, the exact number being difficult to ascertain because of its easy proximity to China and its teeming sampan boat traffic. Something like 98 per cent of the population is Chinese; the occidental population—mostly British, with some Americans and Europeans—is less than 50 thousand. The government is presided over by a governor, appointed by the Crown, and by an Executive Council and a Legislative Council, both nominated (appointed) by the governor. The majority of both councils is Chinese.

What features specially recommend Hong Kong as a tax haven?

It is politically and economically very stable. Some persons knit their eyebrows about the looming presence of Communist China, but Peking has far more to gain with the present situation than from any alteration of it. Hong Kong has traditionally been the gateway to trade with China; and with Communist China's need and desire for trade with the Western nations, Peking would encourage its present status, if anything. That is not to say that China will renew the 99-year lease when it expires in 1997, but there will still be the British sector unless some political change occurs there that is presently unforeseeable. For those persons who are interested in selling to the world's largest population group, Hong Kong is just the spot to be in.

Free enterprise has virtually a free rein in Hong Kong, and the result has been tremendous commercial growth and prosperity. The number of companies registered in Hong Kong is approaching thirty thousand, and they conduct business in all parts of the world as well as in Hong Kong. The rapid growth has been made possible by, and has in turn encouraged, a cooperative spirit by the government. The government's attitude is seen in the continuing free exchange of all currencies, is reflected in the very low taxes for individuals and businesses deriving income from Hong Kong sources, and by a total absence of taxes for companies and individuals conducting their business offshore. The Chinese in the large business community all speak, read, and write English as well as Chinese. English, in fact, with Chinese is the official language and actually takes precedence in government matters and in business. Moreover, because it is an English common-law country, it is an excellent place in which to base a trust. These features, along with its first class harbor, its location on the main trade routes, its large supply of inexpensive labor, its position in the midst of huge populations, its extensive and modern facilities, and wealth of professional talent—all these factors, attracting and fed by a huge influx of investment capital, have made Hong Kong the leading business center among tax havens and the leading tax haven among business centers.

Not only is the climate particularly conducive to business, its very reputation as a manufacturing and trade metropolis gives it a unique advantage over other tax havens and financial centers. Internal Revenue will not be nearly so suspicious of a Hong Kong company's real purpose as it might of a company situated elsewhere. This point actually is what qualifies it more than any other for special consideration among tax haven shoppers.

Facilities. Hong Kong communication and transportation facilities are the equal of any others in the world. Communications include first-class telephone, telegram, cable, and telex systems; radio and television broadcasting; publishing and publications distribution. For giant multinational corporations and large trusts. Among the seventy-five or more banks operating in Hong Kong are branches of the world's largest, including Chase Manhattan, First National City Bank, and other American banks, and banks and trust companies of the major nations in Europe and Asia. With an increasing population, a business turnover of many billions of dollars, free monetary exchange, and an international reputation as a trading center, it's no wonder that virtually every leading bank in the free world maintains at least one branch there.

As we suggested for the Cayman Islands, your agent is already doing business with several banks and can handle the details for you. Once again, we suggest that it not be wiinvestors in the stock market, Hong Kong has four stock exchanges. Transportation means ocean liners and freighters and major airlines on frequent schedules to and from all points on the globe.

Services. Here also, Hong Kong qualifies for handling the most complicated and sophisticated of business enterprises. There are hundreds of law and accounting firms in practice there, the great majority of them involved in handling the affairs of the many companies and trusts. These range from small companies and trusts to giant multinational corporations and large trusts. Among the seventy-five or more banks operating in Hong Kong are branches of the world's largest, including Chase Manhattan, First National City Bank, and other American banks, and banks and trust companies of the major nations in Europe and Asia. With an increasing population, a business turnover of many billions of dollars, free monetary exchange, and an international reputation as a trading center, it is no wo nder that virtually every leading bank in the free world maintains at least one branch there.

As we suggested for the Cayman Islands, your agent is already doing business with several banks and can handle the details for you. Once again, we suggest that it not be with a bank that is headquartered in your own country.

We can also recommend an agent to handle the organization of your Hong Kong company and whatever operational details you wish. He can advise you on the organization of your company and its investments, can take care of the documents you will need, provide nominee directors, nominee shareholders, corporation secretary and perhaps even find an existing dormant or operating company for you to buy if you would rather not set up a new one. The name and address are:

Aall & Zyleman Co., Ltd.
903 T.C. Building
166-168 DesVoux Road Central
Hong Kong, B.C.C.
Phone 5-444180 & 5-444190
CABLE-ALZYLCO

Aall and Zyleman has clients from many different countries, including a number from the United States. The company corresponds in several languages including English, French, German, Dutch, Japanese and Chinese.

As a lecturer, professor, businessman, one of the principals is widely known throughout the financial world and has been engaged in his present business for many years. This firm is not connected with any other institution so you may enjoy maximum security and privacy with their assistance. While on the matter of security, Hong Kong has no tax treaties with other countries requiring detailed tax information and its government supports the protection of privacy in business.

Taxes. There are *no taxes* for a corporation or trust registered in Hong Kong and doing business *outside* the Colony.

Taxes are levied on net profits derived on activities *within* Hong Kong and even these are low in comparison with other countries.

Salaries earned *in Hong Kong* are taxed up to a maximum of 16 1/2 per cent; profits earned in Hong Kong (i.e. buying and selling real estate or operating a shop in Hong Kong) are taxed at 15 per cent of the net after depreciation (dividends are not taxes); interest tax is 15 per cent on anything above 4 per cent a year; and property tax is 16 1/2 per cent on the assessed value of land and buildings with certain exemptions and allowances. There is also a small tax on imports and exports to pay for the promotion of trade, and there are stamp duties on various transactions. Otherwise, even the local population pays no taxes—no capital taxes, wealth taxes, capital gains taxes, gift taxes, or sales taxes. There are duties, however, on a few items such as liquor and tobacco, and these are in effect sales taxes.

Requirements for starting and running a Hong Kong company.

1. *The name* of your company. You will need first, second, and third choices in case of conflict with the same or similar name among Hong Kong companies.

2. Whether to use *nominee directors*. At least two directors are needed, and your agent can provide them for you. The law requires that you have at least one resident director or officer, so probably the second one is worth the privacy that both will give you.

3. *Authorized capital* of your company. A private corporation (in Hong Kong a public corporation is one that sells shares on the open market) does not need any minimum amount, but most capitalize for H.K. $5,000 (U.S. $1,000). It can be expressed in any currency. You will also have to stipulate the par value of shares. (Ten at U.S. $100 each? The more shares, the higher the cost of printing the certificates.) At least two persons must subscribe to the memorandum and the articles of association, and each must hold a minimum of one share. These can be your nominee directors.

4. *The memorandum and articles* will have to be printed. Your agent will handle this for you. As in other countries, the memorandum will contain:

a. the name of the company and its local office address.

b. the purposes of the business.

c. authorized capital, number of shares and par value of each.

d. the names of two officials who have subscribed to the required amount (normally one each) of shares.

The articles of association will probably be more detailed than the bylaws of a U.S. corporation; but like them, they will contain the names of shareholders and directors, the officers and their duties, the scheduling and holding of meetings (director and shareholder meetings can be held anywhere in the world).

5. *Each year, your books will be audited* (or an auditor will sign that they have been audited), and the report will be distributed among shareholders with a copy to Registrar of Companies. This report need not contain benefiriary shareholders' names, and the information is not made public. The audit must be signed by a chartered accountant just as the memorandum and articles must be signed by an accredited Hong Kong lawyer.

6. Your agent can also provide your seal, post the name of your company (required) on a display board in his office, open your bank account for you, and perform whatever duties you wish.

7. *Costs.* Costs will vary depending on how much help you require to set up and run your business, what your capital will be, number of shares issued, number of directors, and so on. Special arrangements have been made for readers of this book whereby costs are substantially lower than available through any other Hong Kong source. It can cost as much as $1500 and up. However, by using the form on the following page you can set up and run a small company at bargain rates as follows:

Registration Cost

1.	Formation and registration of corporation with limited liability of the shareholders.	U.S. $ 80.00
2.	Corporate Seal.	$ 22.50
3.	1 copy of memorandum and articles.	$ 2.50
4.	Annual charge for registered agent service.	$ 50.00
5.	Annual charge for audit report (minimum).	$ 40.00
	Total	**$195.00**

Other Costs:

A. Shares issued in nominee names is at $5.00 per annum for each block of shares.

B. Add $1.50 for each share to be issued for printing and stamp duty.

C. Add $15.00 for each nominee resident director or officer to be provided.

Thus your initial first year minimum cost is only $225.00 for a corporation with 2 nominee directors.

Thereafter your minimum annual cost will be:

Registered Agent	$ 50.00
2 Nominee Directors	$ 30.00
Government Stamp Fee	$ 5.00
Annual Audit Report (minimum)	$ 43.00
TOTAL	**$130.00**

The agent will mail a detailed listing of services available upon request.

In no tax haven with benefits approaching those of Hong Kong is it possible to keep these costs at such remarkably low levels.

Cost of a Trust. The cost for forming a trust varies and depends largely upon your requirements. Your agent can advise you on the form of a trust most suitable for your particular purpose, or if you know precisely what type of trust your purpose requires, your agent will be in a position to determine the ultimate cost.

The drafting of a proper trust deed, which is not out of the ordinary, costs approximately U.S. $200— The annual costs and charges again depend upon the extent of the trust. The minimum annual costs of a Trust amount to U.S. $50.—or one-tenth of one percent of the listed amount of the Trust.

Other Useful Information. All correspondence with your agent should be sent *airmail*. Airmail reaches Hong Kong in about three days from all major cities in the U.S. Your agent can, if you so desire, arrange for an address in the U.S. (on the West coast) to which you can direct your instructions, etc.

When transferring monies between you and your agent, upon request, your agent can arrange forthe utmost privacy through its non-American branch of a wellknown and highly reputable European bank with which the agent maintains accounts.

Tax Haven Factors An Overview (For non-resident companies or Trusts)	Andorra	Antigua	Bahamas	Barbados	Bermuda	Br. Virgin Is.	Cayman Is.	Channel Is.	Costa Rica	Gibraltar	Grenada	Hong Kong	Ireland	Isle of Man	Liberia	Liechtenstein	Luxembourg	Monaco	Montserrat	Netherlands	Neth. Antilles	New Hebrides	Panama	St. Vincent	Singapore	Switzerland	Turks & Caicos
No Tax			x		x		x								x							x					x
No tax foreign source									x	x		x		x	x	x							x				
Low tax	x	x		x		x		x		x								x	x		x		x				
Best for trusts		x	x	x	x	x	x			x	x	x									x		x				x
Best for holding cos.																x	x			x	x					x	
Best for shipping cos.															x								x				
No exchange control	x				x						x				x	x	x						x	x		x	x
No tax treaties			x		x			x		x					x								x	x			x
U. S. tax treaty		x		x		x						x					x		x		x				x	x	
Available no-tax guarantee		x	x	x		x			x					x													
Speak English mainly		x	x	x	x	x	x	x		x	x	x	x	x	x				x			x		x			x
Best facilities		x	x	x		x			x		x	x					x			x			x			x	
Proximity to U.S. & Can.		x	x	x	x	x	x		x		x								x		x		x	x			x
Proximity to Europe	x							x		x			x	x		x	x	x		x						x	
Proximity to Japan												x										x			x		
Banking secrecy*			x		x											x							x	x		x	
Bearer shares available			x			x		x								x						x	x			x	
No financial disclosure															x								x				
Best retirement	x								x														x				
Numbered bank accts.			x									x											x		x	x	

This chart is designed for the purpose of a quick comparison of Tax Havens. For more complete detailed information see section of book that deals with any particular haven.

* These havens have formal bank secrecy laws. However, all Tax Haven banks protect identity of depositors.

CONFIDENTIAL APPLICATION FORM
(Supply to Agent in Duplicate)

To: Address to Agent

Formation of a Company—Application Form   Date _____

---

1. Name of applicant: _____
2. I wish to incorporate: an ordinary company _____
                                       an exempt company _____
3. Name of company: First choice: _____
                                     Second choice: _____
                                     Third choice: _____
4. Purpose of company: _____
_____

5. Name, address, telephone, and cable of each beneficial owner (if more space is needed, write on separate paper, and attach to this form): _____
_____
_____

6. I'd like you to provide: _____
    (how many) nominee directors[1]: _____
    (how many) nominee shareholders: _____ (what)   officers: _____
7. If "none" for nominee directors, give names and addresses of directors[1]: _
8. If "none" for nominee officers, give titles, names and addresses: _____
_____

9. Authorized capital will be: U.S. $ _____ divided among _____
    shares of par[2] value U.S. $ _____ (if this is left blank lowest cost minimum will be provided) _____ Please issue _____
(how many) shares to[3]: _____
10. Bank reference letter for each beneficial owner enclosed from: _____
_____

11. Please open bank account in company name: Yes _____ No _____
    Name of preferred bank: _____
    Names of Signatories, if no nominees required: _____
    (bank reference letter required for each)
12. The following are special instructions: _____
_____

13. I enclose a check in the amount of: _____

Please send me an application form for a trust. My goals are to _____

_____

(use separate sheet if not enough space)

I am enclosing (U.S.) $ _____ to cover registration fee

Signature _____

1. Two directors recommended
2. Par value required for ordinary company only; optional for exempted.
3. Bearer shares available for exempt company only.

All Fees Subject To Change Without Notice

CONFIDENTIAL INFORMATION FORM
(Supply this form to Agent in Duplicate)

To: Aall & Zyleman Co., Ltd.
    903 T. C. Bldg.
    166-168 DesVoux Rd. Central
    Hong Kong, BCC

Formation of a Company—Application Form   Date _____

1. Name of applicant: _____
2. Name of company: First choice: _____
                 Second choice: _____
                 Third choice: _____
3. Purpose of company: (Please be specific) _____

4. Name, address, telephone, and cable of each beneficial owner (if more space needed, write on separate paper, label it, and attach to this form): _

5. Authorized capital*: _____ no shares: _____ per value each*: _____
   (If left blank lowest cost minimum will be used)
6. I wish Aall & Zyleman Co., Ltd. to provide: _____
   (how many) nominee directors: _____
   (how many) nominee shareholders: _____ (what)   officers: _____
7. If "none" for nominee directors, give names and addresses of directors: _

8. If "none" for nominee officers, give titles, names and addresses: _____

9. Personal reference: _____
   Bank reference: _____
   Business reference: _____
   (Supply personal letter copies separately)
10. Please open bank account** in company name: Yes _____ No

   Forward _____ Hold _____ bank statements
   Forward _____ Hold for instructions _____ checks and mail
11. Name and Address of your Bank _____
12. Special instructions: _____

13. I would like to form a Hong Kong Trust—please send me forms. My goals
    are: _____
    _____
    _____

    I am enclosing (U.S.) $ _____ to cover registration fee
                    Legal Signature: _____
* If capital is in excess of U.S. $1000 add $3.00 for each additional $1,000 for
   stamp fees.
**If bank account will be active this service rendered free of charge. If the
   account will be inactive banks will charge opening fee.

All Fees Subject To Change Without Notice

*

BIBLIOGRAPHY

Breen, Quentin L., and Wolf, Douglas H., UNITED STATES LAW AND PRACTICE, Butterworth and Co., Ltd., 88 Kingsway, London WC2, England (1975)

CAYMAN ISLANDS BANK AND TRUST COMPANY DIREC-TORY, International Directories, Ltd., Suite 501 Rivergate Plaza, 44 Brickel Avenue, Miami, Florida 33131 (1975)

THE CAYMAN ISLANDS HANDBOOK AND BUSINESSMAN'S GUIDE, The Northwester Company, Ltd., P.O. Box 243, Grand Cayman, British West Indies (1975)

CHANGING TIMES, The Kiplinger Washington Editors, Inc., Editors Park, Maryland 20782 (July, 1975)

Ellis, Royan D., FINANCIALLY FLEXIBLE CAYMAN ISLANDS, Tax Executives Institute, Inc., Washington, D.C. (1974)

ENCYCLOPEDIA BRITANNICA, Chicago, London, Toronto

Grundy, Milton, GRUNDY'S TAX HAVENS, Third Edition, The Bodley Head, Ltd., and (HFL Publisher Ltd.), London, England (1974)

Langer, Marshall J., HOW TO USE FOREIGN TAX HAVENS, Practicing Law Institute, 810 Seventh Avenue, New York, New York, 10019 (1975)

Langer, Marshal J., and Walker, W.S., THE CAYMAN ISLANDS—A NEW BASE FOR FOREIGN COMPANIES AND TRUSTS, Prentice-Hall, Inc., Englewood Cliffs, New Jersey 07632 (1971)

McKeever, James, MCKEEVER'S MULTINATIONAL INVEST-MENT AND SURVIVAL LETTER, JALCO Survival

Services, Ltd., 726 Richards Street, Vancouver, B.C., Canada (1975)

THE PANAMA CORPORATION IN MULTINATIONAL OPERATIONS, Investors Fiduciary Service Corporation, Apartado 7292, Panama 5, Republica de Panama (1972)

Pick, Franz, THE NUMBERED ACCOUNT, Third Edition, Pick Publishing Corporation, New York, New York 10006 (1972)

Siegel, Edward, DEFEND YOURSELF!, Fawcett World Library (1973)

Starchild, Adam and Finchley, Alan, TAX HAVENS: WHAT THEY ARE AND HOW THEY WORK, Financial Technology Limited, 23 River Road, North Arlington, New Jersey 07032 (1975)

TAX HAVEN REVIEW, Scan Edit A/S, Kompagni, Str. 6, DK-1208, Copenhagen K, Denmark (1975)

SEVENTEEN TAX HAVENS FOR AMERICANS, Kokusai Hatsumei Kaihatsu Kyokai, Ltd.

THE TRUTH ABOUT SWISS BANKING, Swiss Bank Corporation, Basle and Zurich, Switzerland; Swiss Credit Bank, Zurich; Union Bank of Switzerland, Zurich

YOU AND THE LAW, THE READER'S DIGEST Association, Inc., Pleasantville, New York

INDEX

The Nicholas
President's Letter

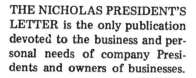

*Business and personal
planning ideas exclusively for the corporation president*

Ted Nicholas has helped many thousands form corporations easily and inexpensively. Now he has organized a brand new service.

THE NICHOLAS PRESIDENT'S LETTER is the only publication devoted to the business and personal needs of company Presidents and owners of businesses.

Will THE NICHOLAS PRESIDENT'S LETTER be useful to every company President? Probably it will. But less so for Presidents of giant corporations like General Motors and U.S. Steel who have large staffs to help them with every problem. This new publication is for Presidents of medium-sized and small companies. These, we believe, are the men and women who need guidance — especially if their company is growing, or just starting up.

This letter provides twice-monthly (24 issues yearly) business and personal guidance for the entrepreneur.

Subjects covered include:

- Investigating new businesses: Ten questions you must ask.

- New ways to raise money for risk capital ... for expansion.

- Expanding your present business. When it's better not to grow.

- Does your business lend itself to mail order? How to find out—for very little money.

- Health care: You can make it all tax-deductible.

- Hiring the right people. How to fire the wrong ones. Ways a small business can attract better people—even against big-company competition.

- Taking full advantage of corporate tax benefits.

- Barter arrangements: They can save you big money. But watch out for two pitfalls.

- Launching your company while you still keep your present job.

- Tax loopholes: A continuing service prepared specifically for company Presidents and owners of small businesses.

- When your competitors are richer and bigger, you can still do nicely. How to make your competition work for you -- no matter what they do!

- Guaranteed ways to pay less in Social Security taxes — and maybe pay nothing at all.

- Travel: how to go first class, and pay less. Spots still unspoiled. How to make sure that every trip for you and your spouse is tax deductible.

- How to fight city hall -- and win. Times when it's better not to fight.

- Ways to minimize customer resistance if you are forced to raise prices.

- The government regulations a President must observe -- broken down according to the size of your business. Regulations you can probably ignore.

- Accounting for Presidents. What to ask your accountant. How to pick the right accountant for your business. Are your accounting fees too high? How to determine if your accountant is giving you the best tax advice.

Also included are:

In depth reports on broader subjects — For instance the energy crunch -- how does the alert President cope with and even profit from it.

Sometimes the in depth reports continue for several issues -- as long as it takes to give all the needed information. If you commissioned such a report from a research organization, you would of course have to pay several thousand dollars for it minimum. (One such report will pay for The Nicholas President's Letter far into the next century!)

Questions and Answers — The editors and outside experts will answer your business and personal questions (without publishing your name, if you prefer privacy.) Here again no need to pay an expensive consultant.

President's Profile — This will portray Presidents who a) are successfully coping with the same problems that are probably plaguing you, and b) are willing to give their fellow Presidents the benefit of their ideas.

You risk nothing. You may cancel The Nicholas President's Letter any time during the life of your subscription. If you do you'll receive a prompt and courteous refund for the unused portion of your subscription.

You will receive an issue -- twice a month, 24 issues a year. The purchase price is tax deductible.

To subscribe mail coupon below. Order today without obligation.

To: The Nicholas President's
Letter
c/o Enterprise Publishing Co.
Enterprise Plaza
Dept. QP - 01N
Two West Eighth Street
Wilmington, DE 19801

Enclosed is ☐ my check or money order for $150.
Charge my ☐ Master Charge
☐ Visa
Card No. _____

_____

Exp. Date _____

Signature _____

Name _____

Company _____

Address _____

City _____ State _____ Zip _____

The Most Astonishing Business Breakthrough of the Decade

Success in business — especially in your own business — is not easy. It takes hard work and it takes knowledge.

You can get help from books and cassettes. And many of them can be of assistance. Now you can have the help of a dynamic business course you can put to work for yourself without risk.

This unique course was developed through years of trial and effort. The author, Ted Nicholas, made . . . and lost . . . two fortunes before refining these techniques into the practical system that built his first million dollar company. The same system can build *your* fortune in less time than you ever thought possible.

You'll learn how to start a business without risking one cent of your money . . . How to turn a hobby into a business . . . Foolproof techniques for immediately sizing up the profit potential of a business for creating money making advertisements . . . For competing against larger companies . . . For choosing the best price for your product or service . . .Choose a business that will prosper during periods of inflation and recession. Here is a partial list of what you will receive with this dynamic course.

The dynamic OPPORTUNITIES UNLIMITED course-between-covers features:

- 22 complete information-packed study-at-home sections . . .
- Self-testing workshop sessions after every section . . .
- Actual tear-out worksheets you can use in setting up your business . . .
- Clear, concise, to-the-point language . . .
- Easy-to-understand charts and diagrams . . .
- More than 500 large, format pages . . .
- Handsome, durable, hardcover bindings . . .

Here's an advance preview of OP-PORTUNITIES UNLIMITED's contents:

- Section One: The Basic Principles. The primary secrets of success.
- Section Two: Starting Your Business Career. Includes the four myths you have to un-learn before you can begin a successful business.
- Section Three: 12 Gripes That Could Be Turned into Business Opportunities. You can put any one of these to use right now--or come up with your own!
- Section Four: Adding the Missing Ingredients. Shows you how to improve on any readily available product—and build a successful business around it.
- Section Five: Specialized Markets. How to make them work for you.
- Section Six: 10 Businesses Started by Solving Problems of Other Businesses. Reveals the secrets of America's most successful entrepreneurs.
- Section Seven: 10 Fortune-Making Opportunities in the Next 25 Years. Tells you how to spot to-

morrow's million-dollar business today.

- Section Eight: Essential Factors to be Considered in Selecting a Business.
- Section Nine: Planning Your Company's Goals and Image. Shows you exactly how to plan the all-important Business Plan. (Complete worksheets included.)
- Section Ten: Legal Considerations for Getting Started. Save $1000s by following these simple guidelines on when you don't need a lawyer.
- Section Eleven: Methods of Starting a Business--Including Part-Time, Franchising and Buying Out. Find out which method is best for you.
- Section Twelve: Financing Your Business. Little-known sources revealed.
- Section Thirteen: Sources of Business Information. Many are actually free!
- Section Fourteen: Bookkeeping and Accounting. It's easier than you ever imagined—when we show you how. (Complete worksheets included.)

- Section Fifteen: Control of Assets. Techniques to make your company grow fast.
- Section Sixteen: Profit Control. How to predict profits in advance of sales.
- Section Seventeen: Financial Leverage. Demonstrates the powerful technique known as "Super Leverage"—and many more proven profit builders.
- Section Eighteen: Personnel Leverage. How to create your own organization from the ground up. (Complete worksheets included.)
- Section Nineteen: Marketing Leverage. How to advertise—guaranteed ideas.
- Section Twenty: Tax Guidelines for Business. Dynamic money-saving methods for minimizing the bracket at which income is taxed-and much, much more.

OPPORTUNITIES UNLIMITED: the only business course-between-covers that guides you step by step —from the drawing board stage to an established business. Now available for a thirty-day Trial Period.

There is nothing else like it available today. The Opportunities Unlimited course offers a uniquely dynamic approach to a business based upon:
One-step-at-a-time guidance, clearly written and concisely presented. We'll take you from your present situation into a new business with specific start-to-finish instruction, and plain-spoken language that's free of jargon and "gobbledegook."

Easy-to-understand examples to illustrate each principle. We won't just tell you how to put your business on the road to success- we'll show you . . . . . with examples drawn from real business situations.

Actual 'workshop" sessions to measure your progress. Each section in your course-between-covers ends with an actual "work" session that will begin to create in you the skills, knowledge, and mind for business so necessary for success.

You CAN make a fortune by starting your own business—send for Opportunities Unlimited now and find out how!

Isn't it time you got started in your own business? Is there anything gained by waiting another minute?

I know from experience that you can do it. And I also know that if you don't take that first big step forward right now, you probably will never do it. Not tomorrow. And maybe not ever.

The decision is now yours to make. Our money-back guarantee is ironclad. There is absolutely no risk of any kind on your part.

You can order Opportunities Unlimited from Enterprise Publishing Company with the form provided on the following pages. The price for the comprehensive course is $85.00. Code 414.

Books for Success

Now Available from Enterprise. . .

OUR LATEST RELEASES

How To Win The Battle Against
Inflation With A Small Business
Creative proven strategies for the
entrepreneur or investor.

*by Franz Serdahley and
Murray Miller, M.D.*

Who *will* survive inflation? This
book answers questions and makes
some startling predictions so impor-
tant for today's future-oriented entrepreneur or investor. Find out what
jobs will come through this unsettled fiscal period, what sections of the
United States will be better equipped financially and physically to with-
stand the shocks of financial "earthquakes." Learn which businesses are
inflation proof and how the self-employed businessperson can come
through this period still owning a major equity in his/her business, with
savings guarded.

Here's a book that thoroughly defines and examines inflation and its
effects on business. Learn why a privately-owned business is the best inflation hedge. The do's and don'ts are practical and easy to understand.
The book contains sound, logical advice without wild promises . . . . .
knowledge and motivation to enable you to make profitable decisions.
Shows how the average individual can improve his/her financial position
through prudent choices and small business opportunities. Covers the
spectrum of investment possibilities.

Hardbound 8½x11

Code 418
Price $14.95

How To Do Your Own Accounting
For A Small Business
by Robert R. Milliron

No need to pay high prices for an
accountant. Shows how to set up a
simple accounting system in easy-to-
understand language. If you thought
you couldn't be your own accountant,
read this and think again.

Continued next page

This book is important because of its simplicity. The author adds interest by using examples that are applicable, enlightening and easy to follow. The language of accounting is basic to wise business decisions whether you own a business or handle the funds for a family. A proper understanding of basic accounting will result in sounder management decisions .

Hardbound 8½ x 11   Code 415
                                                                                          Price $9.95

How To Do Your Own Accounting
Practice Manual

Test your progress chapter by chapter with this companion workbook. This practice manual when used along with the text will give you a complete do-it-yourself home study course in one very inexpensive package.

Paperbound 8½ x 11   Code 303
                                                                                          Price $5.95

SPECIAL COMBINED PRICE FOR THE SET: $14.95   Code 416

How To Advertise:
A Handbook For The Small Business
by Sandra Linville Dean

A useful tool that can be used by the layman to cut through the mystery, learn the jargon and acquire knowledge of the basic principles of advertising. This book was designed and written for the small business operator who knows the necessity of advertising but nothing about the vast possibilities or even how to get started.

This book will enable you to deal with the subject intelligently and when possible, *save money* by taking care of much that's needed without costly agency fees.

You'll learn • Why it pays to advertise • Why your company image is important and how to develop it • Why, when and how to use all media effectively — newspaper, magazines, television, radio, billboards, direct mail, telephone, co-ops — nothing has been left out! • How to plan your advertising budget and campaign and • How to select and work with an agency.

No business owner starting out can afford to be without this dynamic new book!

Hardbound 6 x 9   Code 417
                                                                                          Price $12.95

Here's Good News...
We've Gone Paperback!
Now you can buy our entire library of "How To" help books completely revised and updated and at a FRACTION OF THE COST!

How To Do Business Tax Free
by Midas Malone
How to use the tax havens of the world to personal advantage — Switzerland, Hong Kong, Liechtenstein, Cayman Islands, Panama, Bahamas, Bermuda, and many more are covered with complete explanations. The facts are outlined in detail to work for any income level. Useable forms, names to contact and a complete cost breakdown of trusts and corporations are included.
Quality Paperback 5½ x 8½
Code 305   Price $4.95

Increase Your Take-Home Pay
Up to 40%
by Ted Nicholas
Formerly entitled "The Income Portfolio," this expanded version shows how to convert most any job into a corporation. Enables the user to increase take-home pay up to 40% without a change in job. Employees and employers alike will find this report a useful guide in learning to operate a business with independent contractors. No payroll records or withholding taxes to maintain and it's all in compliance with IRS guidelines. Includes forms and sample letter agreements.
Quality Paperback 5½ x 8½
                                                   Code 306
                                                   Price $2.95

How To Get Out Of Debt
by Ted Nicholas

An aid in developing knowledge for managing financial affairs, personal and business expenses, *and setbacks.* The information applies to all income levels. Bankruptcy and how to get a fresh start is explained and discussed in full detail. This book, formerly entitled "How to Get Out If You're In Over Your Head" has been completely revised to include all new laws pertaining to bankruptcy. Also includes forms and instructions.

Quality Paperback 5½ x 8½

Code 307
Price $4.95

Where The Money Is &
How To Get It
by Ted Nicholas

How and where to raise money to finance a business, scholarship or research grant. Contains hundreds of sources of loans and capital. Complete with names, addresses and telephone numbers. Fully expanded listing includes venture capital firms, state sources, and selected banks. Techniques to save time and produce results. The most comprehensive book of its kind on the market today.

Quality Paperback 5½ x 8½

Code 308
Price $3.95

How To Self-Publish Your Own
Book & Make It A Best Seller
by Ted Nicholas

This very popular book contains all the author's secrets of taking writing to the next step — publishing, marketing and reaping all the rewards of your own book. Covered are all the essentials; reducing production costs, copyrighting, determining selling price, marketing, and how to get free publicity and advertising. This new expanded version includes help with writing, how to get ideas for books, public relations and a complete update on the latest printing processes. Sample letters and forms guide you to the development of your own publishing business.

Quality Paperback 5½ x 8½ Code 309
Price $4.95

How To Form Your Own Corporation Without A Lawyer For Under $50
by Ted Nicholas

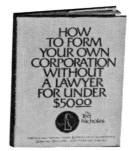

This classic best-selling book provides complete information needed to acquire "The Ultimate Tax Shelter" — your own personal corporation. Explains how to do-it-yourself, without lawyers and at the lowest possible cost. The advantages and disadvantages of incorporation are reviewed to help you decide for yourself.

Provided Is:

- All necessary background information
- The *actual tear-out forms* needed to complete the transaction
- Instructions and samples
- Minutes, bylaws and the *actual certificate of incorporation!*

Hardbound 8½ x 11 Code 401
Price $14.95

Also available in paperback. The forms in this mini-version cannot actually be used, but are available free by sending to the address included within the text.

Quality Paperback 6 x 9 Code 302
Price $5.95

How To Form Your Own Professional Corporation
by Ted Nicholas

In-depth coverage of the subject of incorporation for the *professional* in any field. Reviews the specific advantages and possible disadvantages and explains the important elements to include for efficient planning. Authoritative but easily read, this book provides examples and models of the necessary documents

and includes references and information for additional assistance. Contains tear-out forms, minutes, bylaws and the certificate of incorporation. Everything that's needed.
Hardbound 8½ x 11

Code 407
Price $19.95

Now available in Quality Paperback   6 x 9

Code 310
Price $6.95

Writing Part-time For Fun and Money
by Jack Clinton McLarn

A delightful, witty and charming book on and about writing, fun and money. This is a book that every person with an interest in writing needs at their fingertips. It will be a constant source of useful suggestions, moral support and inside information that no writer should be without. Loaded with personal anecdotes from the author's own experience as a prolific freelance writer. It covers:

- 'Writing for Children and Kids" • Scripts • Reports • Articles
- Greeting Cards • Confessions (or "Confessex" according to the author!)
- And much, much more.

A Great Gift Book
Hardbound 5½ x 8½

Code 412
Price $9.95

In Paperback Too!
Quality Paperback 5½ x 8½

Code 311
Price $3.95

Total Glow:
Dr. Rona's Unbeatable Health Program
by Luanne Rona, M.D.

This is the doctor's system for super health, developed and tested over many years of clinical observations. This is a helpful book for deskbound executives. It's a proven fact that the healthier you are, the more successful. The secrets of achieving super health are revealed in a three-step approach encompassing advanced nutritional concepts, body shaping exercises and exciting new relaxation techniques. It's packed with self-tests and self-improvement worksheets, AND 85 mouthwatering, all natural recipes. The Total Glow system is designed to: • *Stop* premature aging • Help you shed excess weight faster than you thought possible • Increase your energy • Improve your appearance and sex drive.

Hardbound 6 x 9   Code 413
                                                   Price $9.95

Top Secret
(The Enterprise Black Book)
You Are The Author

Blank book, nothing book, write your own book -- and now for your most intimate secrets -- your very own "little black book."

The Enterprise edition of the blank book for your innermost thoughts is 5½" x 8½" hardbound, covered in black linen and gold stamped TOP SECRET.

Hardbound 5½ x 8½   Code 408
                          Price $2.95

How And Where To Raise
Venture Capital To Finance A Business
by Ted Nicholas

How to get the needed funds to start or expand a business. Unusual sources are revealed which are not commonly known, including 227 sources classified by individual to contact, address and telephone number. Information as to how to approach a capital source and various techniques of raising money. Tips to help prepare an effective financial proposal, and to determine start-up costs.

8½ x 11   Code 104
                                     Price $9.95

How To Succeed In Your Own Business
by Ted Nicholas

Recorded live at the State University of New York at Albany, Ted Nicholas conducts a seminar on succeeding in one's own business. The tape is a full 78 minutes of useful, practical advice that listeners can put to immediate use. Contains step-by-step advice on getting a business started and raising capital: picking the right business and where the best opportunities are. An appropriate buy for people of all ages interested in succeeding in business.

Cassette Tape

Code 203
Price $9.95

Satisfaction Guaranteed or Your Money Back

Iron Clad Guarantee --- Complete satisfaction or your money back. If for any reason you are not completely satisfied with an Enterprise Publishing Company product, just return the merchandise undamaged within 14 days and your money will be refunded.

Enterprise Publishing Co., Inc.
Enterprise Plaza, Two West Eighth Street
Wilmington, DE 19801

QP-01X

Name _____

Address _____

City _____

State _____ Zip _____

☐ Check or Money Order Enclosed

Charge my account   Amount _____

☐ Visa   ☐ Master Charge   Exp. Date _____

Card Number _____

Signature _____

YES! Please send me the book(s) listed below. I understand that I may examine the book(s) for 14 days. If I am not fully satisfied for any reason, I may return them undamaged for a full refund of purchase price.

Qty	Code	Title	Price	Total
	104	**(Report)** How And Where To Raise Venture Capital To Finance A Business	9.95	
	203	**(Cassette)** How To Succeed In Your Own Business	9.95	
	302	**(Quality Paperback Books)** How To Form Your Own Corporation Without A Lawyer For Under $50	5.95	
	305	How To Do Business Tax Free	4.95	
	306	Increase Your Take-Home Pay Up To 40%	2.95	
	307	How To Get Out Of Debt	4.95	
	308	Where The Money Is & How To Get It	3.95	
	309	How To Self-Publish Your Own Book & Make It A Best Seller	4.95	

(Please complete both sides of order form)

Cut along this line and mail

	310	How To Form Your Own Professional Corporation	6.95	
	311	Writing Part-time For Fun And Money	3.95	
		(Hardback Books & Courses)		
	401	How To Form Your Own Corporation Without A Lawyer For Under $50	14.95	
	407	How To Form Your Own Professional Corporation	19.95	
	408	Top Secret	2.95	
	412	Writing Part-time For Fun and Money	9.95	
	413	Total Glow	9.95	
	414	Opportunities Unlimited	85.00	
	415	How To Do Your Own Accounting For A Small Business	9.95	
	416	How To Do Your Own Accounting Book and Manual (Set)	14.95	
	417	How To Advertise: A Handbook For The Small Business	12.95	
	418	How To Win The Battle Against Inflation With A Small Business	14.95	
	Total Order			

Note: Publisher pays all postage and handling. Books are shipped 4th class book rate. Allow 4-6 weeks for delivery. For RUSH delivery, first class service...add $1.00 extra per book ordered.

Enterprise Publishing Co., Inc.
Enterprise Plaza, Two West Eighth Street
Wilmington, DE 19801

Cut along this line and mail